P9-AFF-859

# ROAD TRIP USA

## Pacific Coast Highway

1

Jamie Jensen

# Contents

Olympic National Park — pg. 16

Cape Perpetua — pg. 44

Avenue of the Giants — pg. 65

San Francisco — pg. 80

Hearst Castle — pg. 104

San Diego — pg. 134

# PACIFIC COAST HIGHWAY

The amazing thing about the West Coast is that it is still mostly wild, open, and astoundingly beautiful country, where you can drive for miles and miles and have the scenery all to yourself.

# Between Olympic National Park and San Diego, California

**F**or some reason, when people elsewhere in the country refer to the **Pacific Coast**, particularly **California**, it's apparent that they think it's a land of kooks and crazies, an overbuilt suburban desert supporting only shopping malls, freeways, and body-obsessed airheads. All this may be true in small pockets, but the amazing thing about the Pacific Coast—from the dense green forests of western **Washington** to the gorgeous beaches of Southern California—is that it is still mostly wild, open, and astoundingly beautiful country, where you can drive for miles and miles and have the scenery all to yourself.

Starting at the northwest tip of the United States at **Olympic National Park,** and remaining within sight of the ocean almost all the way south to the Mexican border, this 1,500-mile, mostly two-lane route takes in everything from temperate rainforest to near-desert. Most of the Pacific Coast is in the public domain, accessible, and protected from development within national, state, and local parks, which provide habitat for such rare creatures as mountain lions, condors, and gray whales.

Heading south, after the rough-and-tumble logging and fishing communities of Washington State, you cross the mouth of the Columbia River and follow the comparatively peaceful and quiet **Oregon** coastline, where recreation has by and large replaced industry, and where dozens of quaint and not-so-quaint communities line the ever-changing shoreline. At the midway point, you pass through the great redwood forests of Northern California, where the tallest and most majestic living things on earth line the "Avenue of the Giants," home also to some of the best (meaning gloriously kitsch) remnants of the golden age of car-borne tourism: drive-through trees, drive-on trees, houses carved out of trees, and much more. The phenomenally beautiful coastline of Northern California is rivaled only by the incredible coast of

**Big Sur** farther south, beyond which stretch the beachfronts of Southern California. The land of palm trees, beach boys, and surfer girls of popular lore really does exist, though only in the southernmost quarter of the state.

Along with the overwhelming scale of its natural beauty, the West Coast is remarkable for the abundance of well-preserved historic sites—most of which haven't been torn down, built on, or even built around—that stand as vivid evocations of life on what was once the most distant frontier of the New World. While rarely as old as places on the East Coast, or as impressive as those in Europe, West Coast sites are quite diverse and include the Spanish colonial missions of California, Russian and English fur-trading outposts, and the place where Lewis and Clark first sighted the Pacific after their long slog across the continent.

Last but certainly not least are the energizing cities—**Seattle** in the north, **San Francisco** in the middle, and **Los Angeles** and **San Diego** to the south—which serve as gateways to (or civilized respites from) the landscapes in between them. Add to these the dozens of small and not-so-small towns along the coast, with alternating blue-collar ports and upscale vacation retreats, and you have a great range of food, drink, and accommodation options. Local cafés, seafood grills, and bijou restaurants abound, as do places to stay—from youth hostels in old lighthouses to roadside motels (including the world's first, which still stands in lovely San Luis Obispo, California) to homespun B&B inns in old farmhouses.

# WASHINGTON

The coast of Washington is a virtual microcosm of the Pacific Northwest, containing everything from extensive wilderness areas to Native American fishing villages and heavily industrialized lumber towns. Starting at splendid **Port Townsend,** US-101 loops west around the rugged Olympic Peninsula, passing near the northwesternmost point of the continental United States while allowing access to the unforgettable natural attractions—sandy, driftwood-strewn beaches; primeval

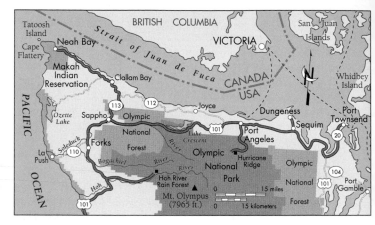

old-growth forests; and pristine mountain lakes and glaciated alpine peaks, to name just a few—of **Olympic National Park.** The roadside landscape varies from dense woods to clear-cut tracts of recently harvested timber, with innumerable rivers and streams perhaps the most obvious signs of the immense amount of rainfall (up to 12 feet) the region receives every year. Scattered towns, from **Port Angeles** in the north to the twin cities of **Grays Harbor** on the coast, are staunchly blue-collar communities almost wholly dependent upon natural resources—not only trees, but also salmon, oysters, and other seafood. Though the tourism trade has been increasing steadily, visitor services are still few and far between, so plan ahead.

Though it's not on the ocean, the Puget Sound port city of Seattle makes a good starting or finishing point to this Pacific Coast road trip.

## Port Townsend

Few places in the world can match the concentration of natural beauty or the wealth of architecture found in tiny **Port Townsend** (pop. 8,727). One of the oldest towns in Washington, Port Townsend was laid out in 1852 and reached a peak of activity in the 1880s. But after the railroads focused on Seattle and Puget Sound as their western terminus, the town sat quietly for most of the next century until the 1960s, when an influx of arts-oriented refugees took over the waterfront warehouses and cliff-top mansions, converting them to galleries, restaurants, and comfy B&Bs while preserving the town's turn-of-the-20th-century character.

Port Townsend is neatly divided into two halves: Multi-story brick warehouses and commercial buildings line Water Street and the wharves along the bay, while lovely old Victorian houses cover the bluffs above. It's basically a great place to wander, but there are a

The Waterstreet Hotel

couple of sights worth seeing, particularly the landmark **City Hall** along the east end of Water Street at 210 Madison Street. Half of this eclectic gothic pile now houses a local historical museum (daily; donations accepted), with three floors of odds and ends tracing Port Townsend history, including the old city jail where Jack London spent a night on his way to the Klondike goldfields in 1897. The City Hall is also a starting point for Joyce Webb's expertly guided walking tours (daily by appointment; 360/385-1967) of the waterfront district.

Not surprisingly, considering the extensive tourist trade, Port Townsend has a number of good restaurants and bars. You'll find many of the best places at the east end of town near the corner of Water and Quincy Streets. For breakfast or lunch, try the **Salal Cafe** (360/385-6532), at 634 Water Street. For lunch or dinner, one of the best seafood places is the **Silverwater Cafe** (360/385-6448), at 237 Taylor Street near the Quincy Street dock. The old waterfront neighborhood also holds a pair of restored 1880s hotels: the **Waterstreet Hotel** ($65 and up; 360/385-5467 or 800/735-9810), above a saloon (with frequent live music) at 635 Water Street, and the quieter **Palace Hotel,** 1004 Water Street ($135

**Fort Worden,** on the north side of Port Townsend, is a retired military base that served as a location for the Richard Gere movie *An Officer and a Gentleman.* It now hosts an excellent series of annual music and arts festivals; contact the Centrum at 360/385-5320 for schedules and more information.

## Toward Seattle: Port Gamble

You have a number of options if traveling to or from Port Townsend. You can follow US-101 around the western Olympic Peninsula, or take a ferry via Whidbey Island and explore it and the even prettier San Juan Islands to the north. Last, but not least, you can take a middle route across the Kitsap Peninsula, then catch a ferry to Seattle.

This last route, which includes a trip on the very frequent (and frequently crowded) Washington State Ferry ($13; 206/464-6400) between Kingston and Edmonds, has the great advantage of taking you through the lovely old logging town of **Port Gamble,** a slice of New England on the shores of Puget Sound. The entire town is a historic district, with dozens of immaculate Victorian buildings standing along maple tree–lined streets. After wandering past the saltbox houses, have a look inside the large General Store, which includes a barber shop, a seashell museum, and a small café; or visit the photo-filled **historical museum** ($2.50; 360/297-8074) across the street.

and up; 360/385-0773), where the room names play up the building's past use as a brothel.

The most comfortable accommodations in Port Townsend are the many 1880s-era B&Bs dotting the bluffs above the port area, including the ever-popular **Old Consulate Inn,** 313 Walker Street ($130 and up; 360/385-6753), where the plush rooms come with a view of Mt. Olympus and a hearty multi-course breakfast. For less-pricey lodging, there's a **campground** (360/344-4400) and the **HI-Olympic Hostel** ($22 per person; 360/385-0655) with dorm beds in the old Army barracks at Fort Worden, on the coast two miles north of town.

The natural cut of the **Hood Canal** on the east side of the Olympic Peninsula is one of the West Coast's prime oyster-growing estuaries, source of the gourmet Quilcenes, Hama Hamas, and other varieties available at roadside stands, shops, and restaurants throughout the region.

### Sequim and Dungeness

A half hour southwest of Port Townsend via Hwy-20 and US-101, **Sequim** (pop. 4,334; pronounced "SKWIM") sits in the rain shadow of the Olympic Mountains and so tends to be much drier and sunnier than spots even a few miles west. Though it retains its rural feel, Sequim's historic farming-and-fishing

The Indian-owned **7 Cedars Casino** stands above US-101 at the foot of Sequim Bay, fronted by totem poles.

economy is quickly switching over to tourism, with tracts of new homes filling up the rolling, waterfront landscape and a new freeway bypassing the center of town. It's ideal cycling country, for the moment at least, with acres and acres of lavender farms lining quiet country roads.

Coming in from the east on two-lane US-101, the first thing you pass is the large, modern **John Wayne Marina,** built on land donated by The Duke himself. The US-101 frontage through town is lined by the usual franchised fastfood outlets and some unique variations, like the 1950s-themed **Hi-Way 101 Diner** (360/683-3388), at 392 W. Washington Street in the heart of town.

Just north of US-101 at 175 W. Cedar Street, the **Sequim-Dungeness Museum** (Tues.–Sun. 8 AM–4 PM; donation; 360/683-8110) houses everything from 12,000-year-old mastodon bones discovered on a nearby farm, to exhibits of Native American cultures and pioneer farm implements. From the museum, a well-marked road winds north for 10 miles before reaching the waterfront again at **Dungeness,** where a seven-mile-long sand spit, the country's longest, protects a shellfish-rich wildlife refuge. All

Sequim's annual **Irrigation Festival,** held every May, is Washington's oldest community celebration.

that remains of the abandoned fishing community that existed here through the 1890s is an old schoolhouse, though the excellent **Three Crabs Restaurant** (360/683-4264), overlooking Dungeness Harbor, has been serving up fresh fish and local Dungeness crab (and gorgeous crab cake "crab-burgers") for over 50 years.

The well-signed **Olympic Game Farm** (daily in summer; $9; 360/778-4295), five miles northwest of Sequim, is a 90-acre retirement home for former animal actors and other creatures, great and small. Visitors are very welcome.

Stay in Sequim at **Groveland Cottage** ($100 and up; 360/683-3565), a quaint B&B just a half mile from the harbor at 4861 Sequim-Dungeness Way, or at the popular waterfront **Juan de Fuca Cottages** ($120 and up; 360/683-4433), two miles to the west at 182 Marine Drive.

# Seattle

An engaging and energetic combination of scenic beauty, blue-collar grit, and high-tech panache has made Seattle one of the most popular cities in the United States, for visitors and residents alike. A young city, historically and demographically, Seattle has managed to preserve much of its heavy industrial heritage as parks and museums, if not as economic engines. The eco-conscious, civic-minded city spreads over a series of hills, surrounded by the waters of Puget Sound (be sure to ride a ferry or two!), with a backdrop of the snow-capped Cascade and Olympic Mountains. The evergreen Seattle can be an entrancing city—at least when the sun comes out, which no matter what people say is likely to happen at least once during your stay.

The heart of downtown Seattle, **Pike Place Market** is a raucous fish, crafts, and farmers market with some 250 different stalls and stores filling a 1930s municipal-feeling building that steps along the waterfront. For a respite from the hubbub, head two blocks south to the postmodern **Seattle Art Museum,** 1300 1st Avenue (closed Mon.; $13; 206/654-3100), and enjoy the amazing collection of regional Native American art and artifacts on display.

The Two Sentries,
The 42 story L. C. Smith Building and Mt. Rainier.
SEATTLE
U.S.A.

Downtown's other piece of noteworthy recent architecture is the shiny **Seattle Central Library** at 1000 4th Avenue, a fantastic (and free!) high-tech (some say hermetic) space whose multifaceted glass diamond exterior steps down between two city blocks.

At the south edge of downtown, a half mile from the Pike Place Market, the 30-block Pioneer Square historic district preserves the original core of the city, which boomed in the late 1890s with the Klondike Gold Rush. Another essential place to go is the **Seattle Center** (206/684-8582), north of downtown at Broad Street and 5th Avenue North, built for the 1962 World's Fair. Take the elevator to the top of the landmark Space Needle or ride the monorail, or Windstorm roller coaster, bumper cars, or a dozen other funfair attractions at the summer-only Fun Forest (noon–midnight; pay-per-ride). The Seattle Center, location for Seattle's excellent annual Labor Day arts and music festival, Bumbershoot, is also home to the intriguing **Experience Music Project** (206/367-5483), a hands-on musical exploration and living memorial to the city's native-born guitar genius, Jimi Hendrix. A don't-miss photo opportunity: A statue of Chief Seattle with the Space Needle rising behind him.

Besides funding the Experience Music Project, Microsoft millionaire Paul Allen has indulged his taste for Space Age adventure by subsidizing the private rocketship SpaceShipOne, and closer to home by renovating the world's last intact **Cinerama Theatre** (206/441-3080), an early 1960s icon at 2100 Fourth Avenue.

Spectators enjoy downtown views and Puget Sound sunsets at SAFECO Field ballpark, south of Pioneer Square, where the **Seattle Mariners** (206/346-4001) play.

## Practicalities

Seattle's main airport is Seattle–Tacoma International ("Sea-Tac"), a half-hour drive south of downtown Seattle via the I-5 freeway. Seattle's freeways are often filled to capacity most of the day, but the best drive-through tour of Seattle follows old US-99 along the Alaska Way Viaduct, a concrete freeway that cuts along the downtown waterfront, runs through a tunnel, then follows Aurora Avenue on a soaring bridge over the Lake Union Canal. (By the way, under the Aurora Bridge sits one of Seattle's biggest pieces of auto-art: the Aurora Troll, caught in the act of eating an old VW Beetle.)

Most everything of visitor interest in Seattle is within the walkably compact downtown, where an extensive bus system runs in a fare-free zone; there's also a mile-long monorail ($1), linking 5th and Pine Streets downtown with the Seattle Center and Space Needle.

The niftiest place to stay is the **Hotel Andra** ($180 and up; 206/448-8600), at 2000 4th Avenue, a fully modernized

1920s hotel three blocks from Pike Place Market. The cheapest place to stay has to be the **HI-Seattle Hostel** (206/622-5443) at 84 Union Street, which offers clean and comfortable dorm beds for around $25, right along the waterfront next to Pike Place Market.

Seafood, not surprisingly, is the thing Seattle restaurants do best, and the city is full of great places to eat fish (the sushi here is as good as it gets, outside Japan). For fish-and-chips or cheap, fresh oysters (and Washington produces more oysters than anywhere else in the United States), head down to **Emmett Watson's Oyster Bar** (206/448-7721) at the north end of Pike Place Market. More down-home fare is served up for breakfast, lunch, and dinner at the **5 Spot** (206/285-7768), at 1502 Queen Anne Avenue in the residential Queen Anne district, a mile northwest of downtown high above Lake Union.

The best source of advance information on visiting Seattle is the Seattle Convention and Visitors Bureau (206/461-5840).

Pike Place Market

## Port Angeles

A busy, industrial city at the center of the northern Olympic Peninsula, **Port Angeles** (pop. 18,397) makes a handy base for visiting the nearby wilderness of Olympic National Park. The town is slowly but surely recovering from its traditional dependence on logging, and the waterfront, which once hummed to the sound of lumber and pulp mills, is now bustling with tourists wandering along a six-mile walking trail and enjoying the sealife (sea slugs, eels, starfish, and octopuses) on display at the small but enjoyable **Marine Life Center** (daily; $2.50), on the centrally located City Pier.

Weather on the Olympic Peninsula varies widely from place to place. The peaks and coastal valleys of **Olympic National Park** receive as much as 200 inches of rainfall each year, while the town of **Sequim**, a mere 30 miles away, garners an average of just 17 inches annually.

Malls, gas stations, and fast-food franchises line the US-101 frontage through town, but life in Port Angeles, for locals and visitors alike, centers on the attractive downtown area, two blocks inland from the waterfront around Lincoln Avenue and 1st Street. Here cafés like **First Street Haven** (360/457-0352), at 107 E. 1st Street, offer good, inexpensive soup-and-salad lunches and dinners, and amiable bars and pubs like **Peaks,** around the corner at 130 S. Lincoln Avenue (360/452-2802), draw bikers, hikers, and loggers with their pub grub and good beers (99 bottles, plus some intriguing "home brews"). If

### Ferries to Victoria, British Columbia

From Port Angeles, a pair of ferries—the **MV _Coho,_** carrying cars and passengers ($35 per car one-way, plus $13 per person; 360/457-4491), and the faster, summer-only **Victoria Express,** carrying passengers only ($16.50 per person each way; 360/452-8088)—shuttle across the water to and from pretty Victoria, the provincial capital of British Columbia, one of Canada's most popular destinations. Both ships leave Port Angeles at the middle of the attractively landscaped waterfront and arrive very near the center of Victoria, making for a great day trip from either place. At the Port Angeles dock there's a very helpful information center packed with maps and brochures on Victoria and the rest of B.C., or you can call **Tourism Victoria** at 800/663-3883.

## Olympic National Park

Olympic National Park, in the heart of the Olympic Peninsula, is a diversely beautiful corner of the country, combining features of Maine's rocky coast and the snow-capped peaks of the Rocky Mountains with the unique rainforests covering the park's Pacific coastal valleys. The rugged, million-acre landscape, ranging from rocky shores to impassably dense forests, resisted exploitation and development until the turn of the 20th century, when local conservationists persuaded Teddy Roosevelt to declare most of the peninsula a nature preserve, a movement that eventually resulted in the establishment of Olympic National Park in 1939.

There are no roads and few trails across the peninsula, so you have to choose your points of entry depending upon what you want to see. The different areas of Olympic National Park are covered in the surrounding pages, but the most popular part of the park is Hurricane Ridge, which rises high above Port Angeles and offers great views of the silvery peaks and the many glaciers that flank them. (The wildflowers can be spectacular in late spring.)

At the northwestern corner of the park, Lake Crescent sits serenely amidst the forests and peaks, while on the western slopes, the temperate rainforests of the usually wet and rainy river valleys hold some of the world's largest trees, all draped with a thick fabric of mosses. At the western edge of the peninsula, the almost completely undeveloped Pacific Ocean coastline, added to the park in 1953, offers miles of sandy beaches and rocky headlands, littered only with driftwood logs and vibrant tidepools.

you're waiting for a ferry, or are fresh off of one, a number of places to eat and drink surround the ferry terminal, including the attractive **Landings Restaurant** at 115 E. Railroad Avenue (360/457-6768), with great fish-and-chips.

Places to stay in Port Angeles vary. You'll find highway motels, including the **Quality Inn Uptown** ($80 and up; 360/457-9434), at 101 E. 2nd Street, and the **Red Lion**

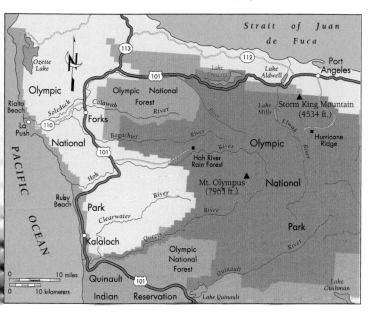

($109–150; 360/452-9215), on the water at the foot of Lincoln Street. There are also many characterful B&Bs; for details on these, and for more general information, phone the **North Olympic Peninsula Visitors and Convention Bureau** at 800/942-4042, or stop by the Port Angeles **tourist office** (360/452-2363) at the ferry terminal, 121 E. Railroad Avenue.

## Hurricane Ridge

High above Port Angeles, **Hurricane Ridge** provides the most popular access to **Olympic National Park.** A paved road twists and turns 17 miles up a steep 7 percent grade to the mile-high summit, where, on a clear day, you can gape at the breathtaking 360-degree views of mountain, valley, and sea. A summer-only lodge at the crest provides food and drink, and a concession offers ski and snowshoe rentals on winter weekends. Trails lead down into the backcountry, where you're likely to spot marmots, deer, and bald eagles—and if you're lucky, maybe an elk or a mountain lion. From Hurricane Ridge, thrill-seeking drivers and mountain bikers may get a kick out of Obstruction Point Road, a twisting gravel road that continues (without guardrails!) for another eight miles along the crest from the parking lot. In winter, the snowed-in road becomes a popular cross-country skiing trail.

Apart from the area right around Hurricane Ridge, most of the Olympic National Park backcountry is fairly wet and rugged. If you plan to camp overnight, be prepared, and be sure to get a permit from the Olympic National Park **visitor center** (360/565-3130) in Port Angeles, two blocks south of US-101 on the road up to Hurricane Ridge. This is also the best place to pick up general information on the rest of the park, which extends all the way west to the rainforest areas along the coastal valleys.

## Lake Crescent

One of the most idyllic spots in the entire Pacific Northwest, the fjord-like **Lake Crescent,** over eight miles long and some 625 feet deep, lies right alongside two-lane US-101, just 20 miles west of Port Angeles. Powerboats are banned, and the placid surface reflects the clouds and surrounding peaks, including 4,534-foot Storm King Mountain; to appreciate the tranquil beauty, rent a rowboat from the Lake Crescent Lodge and float around under your own steam. Starting from the lodge, a popular mile-long hike follows a well-maintained nature trail up to the delicate cascade of 90-foot **Marymere Falls,** while along the north shore an abandoned railroad grade is open to hikers and mountain bikers.

Incomparably situated along US-101 on the lake's southeast shore, **Lake Crescent Lodge** (open April–Oct. only; $120 and up; 360/928-3211) was originally built in 1916 and has been hosting visitors ever since. Fairly rustic rooms are available in the old lodge, which also has a cozy dining room; more modern accommodations are available in the adjacent cabins and motel, though the whole place is booked solid on summer weekends, so reserve as soon as you can. Another nice place to stay is the **Log Cabin Resort** ($120 and up; 360/928-3325), three miles north of US-101 on the "sunny northeast shore," with motel rooms and waterfront A-frame cabins.

In the forested hills above US-101, **Sol Duc Hot Springs Resort** ($90 and up; 360/327-3583) has family-friendly cabins and a restaurant set around a swimming pool and natural hot spring ($11 for non-guests).

## Hwy-112: Strait of Juan de Fuca

The Strait of Juan de Fuca, the narrow inlet that links the open

Pacific with Puget Sound and divides the United States from Canada, was named for the Greek sailor (real name: Apostolos Valerianus) who first mapped it while working for the Spanish Crown in 1610. On a clear day, you can get some great views across the strait from Hwy-112, which runs along the shore from US-101 all the way to the tip of the Olympic Peninsula at Neah Bay. Though it looks like a great drive on the map, Hwy-112 is a very narrow and winding road with some surprisingly steep hills and thick woods that block much of the view, all of which (in addition to the plentiful logging trucks) can make it less than ideal for bicycling or even a scenic drive.

The fish-headed, human-legged, sneaker-wearing statue that stands outside the Clallam Bay General Store is known alternately as "The Running Fish," "Gill," and "The Fishman," for obvious reasons.

## Neah Bay and Cape Flattery

From the crossroads at Sappho on US-101, Hwy-113 leads north, linking up with Hwy-112 on a long and winding 40-mile detour through Clallam Bay (home of the nearly-world-famous *Running Fish* statue) to **Cape Flattery,** the northwesternmost tip of the continental United States. The highway is paved as far as the town of **Neah Bay,** a tiny (population 750) and somewhat bedraggled community that's the center of the Makah Indian Reservation. Salmon and halibut fishing, both by Makah and by visitors, is about the only activity here, though the tribe does have the impressive and modern

In the late 1990s, as part of an effort to preserve tribal traditions and instill pride in younger Makah, the **Makah tribe** resumed small-scale hunting of migratory gray whales, which they had voluntarily ceased when the whales became endangered a century ago. Though the hunting was largely ceremonial, the news raised the hackles of wildlife organizations, which filed lawsuits and staged loud protests to prevent whales from being killed.

**Makah Museum** (daily in summer, closed Mon. and Tues. the rest of the year; $5; 360/645-2711), one of the best anthropological museums in the state. Most of the displays are of artifacts uncovered in 1970, when a mudslide revealed the pristine remains of a 500-year-old coastal village—the Pompeii of the Pacific Northwest. Other galleries display finely

crafted baskets, a full-scale longhouse complete with recorded chants, and a whaling canoe from which fearless Makah harpooners would jump into the surf and sew up the jaws of dying whales, to keep them from drowning and sinking. If you want a special souvenir, the museum gift shop displays and sells a variety of high-quality arts and crafts made by Makah people.

The Hwy-112/113 route twists along the rocky and wooded shore of the Strait of Juan de Fuca, but reaching the actual cape itself isn't difficult. From Neah Bay, the well-maintained western half of the Cape Loop Road winds along the Pacific to a parking area which gives access to a trail that brings you to the top of a 65-foot-high cliff overlooking the crashing surf and offshore **Tatoosh Island.** On a sunny day it's a gorgeous vista, but if the weather's less than perfect (which it often is) your time would be much better spent inside the Makah Museum.

## Forks

Bending southwest along the banks of the Sol Duc River, US-101 passes through miles of green forests under ever-gray skies to reach **Forks** (pop. 3,120), the commercial center of the northwestern Olympic Peninsula. Named for its location astride the Sol Duc and Bogachiel Rivers, Forks is a die-hard lumber town grappling with the inevitable change to more ecologically sustainable alternatives, mainly tourism. Visitors come to fish for steelhead during the late-summer runs, to

The old-growth forests of Olympic National Park provide prime habitat for **the northern spotted owl,** an endangered species whose preservation has sparked heated debate throughout the Pacific Northwest.

beachcomb along the rugged coast, or to visit the remarkable rainforests of Olympic National Park to the southeast. The main attraction in Forks proper is the quirky, summer-only **Timber Museum** (daily; 360/374-9663), on US-101 on the south edge of town, packed with handsaws, chainsaws, and other logging gear as well as antique cooking stoves and displays telling the town's characterful history. There's also a forest-fire lookout tower perched outside the upper floor gallery.

With four gas stations and four motels, Forks is not a metropolis by any stretch of the imagination, but it does offer the best range of services between Port Angeles and Aberdeen. **Sully's** at 220 N. Forks Avenue is a good burger stand on US-101 at the north end of town. There are also two Chinese and two Mexican places, plus the great smoked salmon sandwiches at the **Smoke House Restaurant.** Stay at the **Forks Motel** ($50–90; 360/374-6243), at 351 S. Forks Avenue, or a more peaceful B&B, the **Miller Tree Inn** ($85 and up; 360/374-6806), which sits on 30 acres at 654 E. Division Street, five blocks east of Forks's solitary stoplight.

South of Forks along US-101, **Bogachiel State Park** has over 100 forested acres of very nice campsites (with showers!) along the Bogachiel River. Sites are first-come, first-served, and cost around $10 for tents, $15 for RV hookups (360/374-6356).

For more information, contact the Forks **visitors center** (800/443-6757), next to the Timber Museum.

# Hoh River Rainforest

If you have time to visit only one of the lush rainforest areas of Washington's northwest coast, head for the **Hoh River Rainforest,** 12 miles south of Forks and then 18 miles east along a well-signed and well-paved road. Not only is this the most easily accessible of these incredibly lush, old-growth areas, the Hoh River forest is also among the least disturbed, with a thick, wet blanket of vibrant green ferns, mosses, and lichens covering every inch of the earth at the foot of massive hemlocks, cedars, and towering Sitka spruce. Displays inside the visitors center tell all about the forest's flora

If you're very lucky, you might spy one of the rare **Roosevelt elk,** for whose protection Olympic National Park was established; if you're unlucky, you might also come face-to-face with a mountain lion, which can be dangerous but generally avoids contact with humans.

Ruby Beach

and fauna and how they are affected by the massive rainfall here—upwards of 140 inches every year. There's also a wheelchair-accessible nature trail and a wide range of hiking trails, including the quickest access to the icy summit of 7,965-foot Mt. Olympus, 22 miles away in the glacier-packed alpine highlands at the heart of the park.

The closest services to the Hoh River Rainforest are in Forks, but budget travelers may want to take advantage of the $12-a-night bunks at the amiable **Rain Forest Hostel** (360/374-2270), 23 miles south of Forks along US-101 (between milemarkers 169 and 170), midway between the Hoh River Rainforest and the coast at Ruby Beach.

## Kalaloch and the Pacific Beaches

Looping around the northern Olympic Peninsula, US-101 finally reaches the coast 27 miles south of Forks at **Ruby Beach,** where a series of wave-sculpted sea stacks frame a photogenic, driftwood-strewn cove. From Ruby Cove, US-101 runs south through the wild coastal section of Olympic National Park, which is almost always foggy and cool, even when the weather's sunny and hot just a mile inland. While almost the entire coast south from Cape Flattery is protected within the national park, this is the only easily accessible stretch. Parking areas along the highway, numbered from Beach 6 to Beach 1 north to south, give access to 20 miles of generally deserted beach, backed by rocky bluffs and packed with tidepools, driftwood castles, and an incredible variety of flotsam and jetsam.

At the southern end of this short but sweet stretch of coastline, between Beach 2 and Beach 3, 25 miles north of Lake

Quinault, **Kalaloch Lodge** ($120–250; 360/962-2271) is a modern resort, with a coffee shop and a nice restaurant overlooking a picturesque cove. There's also a gas station, a summer-only **ranger station** across US-101, and an oceanside **campground** just to the north.

## Lake Quinault

Spreading in a broad valley at the southwest corner of Olympic National Park, **Lake Quinault** offers lush rainforest groves within a short walk or drive of most creature comforts. The lake has served for decades as a popular resort destination—cabins, lodges, and stores dating from the 1920s line the southern shore, just outside the park boundary—and the old-growth

> From US-101 at Hoquiam, Hwy-109 runs west and north along the Pacific Ocean through a series of small fishing ports and beach resorts to the heavily logged lands of the **Quinault Indian Reservation.**

forests here have survived intact, though the naked tracts of clear-cut timber along US-101 north and south of the lake give a good sense of what the area might have looked like had Teddy Roosevelt and friends not stepped in to protect it around the turn of the 20th century.

The best first stop is the USFS **ranger station** (360/956-2400) on the south shore, where you can get details of the many excellent hikes in the Lake Quinault area and pick up a map of the guided driving tour around the lake, including the location of the many record-size trees. The roughly four-mile-long **Quinault Loop Trail** winds on a paved path from the ranger station along crashing Cascade Creek up through an old-growth rainforest of alders and bigleaf maples, whose leaves grow upwards of 12 inches across (and provide some splendid "fall color"). Midway along, the trail crosses a raised wooden boardwalk through a fecund cedar swamp, then drops down again along another creek before returning by way of the lakeshore.

On the lakeshore right next to the ranger station, historic **Lake Quinault Lodge** ($150 and up; 360/288-2900) is well worth a look, with a rustic but spacious lobby opening onto lakefront lawns, though the rooms could do with some TLC. The **Rain Forest Resort Village** ($95 and up; 360/288-2535 or 800/562-0948), at the east end of the lake, besides offering comfortable and reasonably priced accommodations (from camping to cabins) and very good food in the Salmon House restaurant, also holds the **World's Largest Spruce,** a 191-foot giant.

## Grays Harbor: Hoquiam and Aberdeen

The Olympic Peninsula is cut off from the southern Washington coast by the spade-shaped bay of **Grays Harbor,** named for the early American sea captain and explorer, Robert Gray. Long the state's prime lumber port, Grays Harbor still processes huge piles of trees, but in many ways what's most interesting is the contrast between the two towns here, Hoquiam and Aberdeen.

At the western end of Grays Harbor, tidy **Hoquiam** (pop. 9,097; kind of rhymes with "requiem") celebrates its lumber-based history with an annual Logger's Playday bash, complete with ax-throwing and tree-climbing competitions, the second weekend in September. The rest of the year, get a feel for the bygone days of the lumber industry at red-shingled **Hoquiam's Castle** (daily; $4; 360/533-2005), on a hillside three blocks off US-101 at 515 Chenault Avenue, a 20-room mansion built in 1897 by a local lumber baron. If you like the looks of it, you can stay overnight: Hoquiam's Castle is also a B&B ($125 and up). Another grand old timber-magnate mansion now houses the **Polson Museum** (Wed.–Sun; $4; 360/533-5862), on US-101 at 1611 Riverside Drive. Not surprisingly, it's devoted to the history of logging.

> Grunge-rock hero and Nirvana lead singer **Kurt Cobain** grew up in and around Aberdeen.

East of Hoquiam along the Chehalis River at the head of Grays Harbor, **Aberdeen** (pop. 16,600) is much more heavily industrialized and thus has been even harder hit by the continuing downturn in the Northwest timber industry. The downtown area has more than a few rough edges, but it also holds one of the more high-profile of the state-sponsored efforts to move from timber to tourism: **Grays Harbor Historical Seaport** (daily; $3; 360/532-8611), a half mile east of US-101. A reconstruction of one of American explorer (and

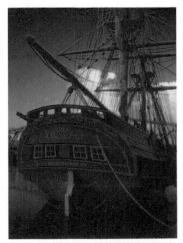

The *Lady Washington* is a replica of one of the first American ships to explore the West Coast.

Grays Harbor namesake) Capt. Robert Gray's ships, the *Lady Washington,* can be toured—when she's not off on one of her regular "goodwill" cruises. The original ship was the first American vessel to visit the area, way back in 1788, and the replica was completed here in 1989 to celebrate the Washington State centennial.

Across the river from Aberdeen, the region's largest employer, a Weyerhaeuser pulp mill, looms alongside US-101 through the inappropriately named town of Cosmopolis, before the road cuts inland toward Raymond and Willapa Bay.

Heading east from Aberdeen, US-12 cuts inland, passing the Satsop nuclear power plant and one of the most heavily logged areas in Washington before joining the I-5 freeway at the state capital of Olympia. Midway along, the **HI-Grays Harbor Hostel** in Elma (360/482-3119) has $14-a-night beds (and a small Frisbee golf course!).

## Hwy-105: Westport and Tokeland

Between Hoquiam and Raymond, US-101 cuts inland from the coast, while an alternative route, Hwy-105, loops to the west past miles of cranberry bogs (and occasional wild elk) through the salmon-fishing town of **Westport.** Once called "The Salmon Capital of the World," and still a prime place for watching migrating gray whales, Westport is a very busy port—and one of Washington's few good surfing, clam-digging, and surf-kayaking beaches. The whole place really comes to life during the Labor Day seafood festival, but any time of the year the best stop is **Brady's Oysters** (360/268-0077), at the foot of the Hwy-105 bridge from Aberdeen.

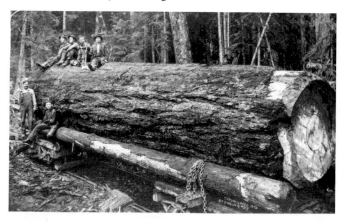

At the south edge of the peninsula, absorb more coastal character at the 120-year-old **Tokeland Hotel** ($65; 360/267-7006), off Hwy-105 on the north shore of Willapa Bay, with old-fashioned lodgings (shared bathrooms) and a very nice dining room.

## Willapa Bay: Raymond and South Bend

One of the country's prime oystering grounds, **Willapa Bay** is sheltered from the Pacific by the Long Beach Peninsula and fed by the Nasalle, Willapa, and North Fall Rivers. There are very few towns or even villages on this stretch of US-101, which winds past tidal marshes, cattle ranches, and extensively clear-cut forests—which billboards proclaim to be "America's first industrial tree farm," giving dates of harvest, planting, and re-harvest, on a roughly 40-year cycle.

If the weather's right for a picnic, **fresh shellfish** can be had at bargain prices—live in the shell, or pre-shucked by the half gallon—from the area's many producers, wholesalers, and roadside stands. Look for them all along US-101 and up the Long Beach peninsula.

At the northeast corner of Willapa Bay, on the south bank of the Willapa River, stand two towns that jointly embody the natural resource–based history and economy of the Pacific Northwest: **Raymond** (pop. 2,975) has the lumber mills, while **South Bend** (pop. 1,807) calls itself the "Oyster Capital of the World." South Bend's other claim to fame is its landmark **Pacific County Courthouse** (Mon.–Fri. only), which since 1910 has loomed like a mini Taj Mahal on a hill just east of US-101. Step inside for a look at the 30-foot stained-glass dome above the rotunda, and wander through the lushly landscaped park next door.

If you want to stretch your legs, Raymond and South Bend are linked by a nice walking and cycling path, which follows an old railroad right-of-way along the Willapa River, amidst some engaging roadside sculptures of people canoeing, bird-watching, cycling, fishing, and generally enjoying the Great Outdoors.

## Long Beach Peninsula

On the western side of Willapa Bay, the **Long Beach Peninsula** stretches for 28 miles of hard-packed sandy beaches along the roiling Pacific Ocean. Away from the few small towns, beaches and breakers abound along here, and you won't have any problem finding peace and solitude. The center of activity on the Long Beach Peninsula is the town of **Long Beach,** two miles from US-101, with a wanderable collection of crafts galleries and souvenir shops. A short walk west from "downtown" Long Beach, a wooden boardwalk winds along the coastal dunes, and a short trail leads to a very rare sight: the reconstructed skeleton of a gray whale. Lewis and Clark saw similar bones when they passed by 200-plus years ago, and a "Discovery Trail" linking "corps and Discovery" locations runs from here

"World's Largest Frying Pan"

south to Ilwaco, near the mouth of the Columbia River.

If you can bear to stretch your budget a little, Long Beach is home to one of the coast's best B&Bs, the historic **Shelburne Inn** ($150 and up; 360/642-2442), located in the Seaview neighborhood at Pacific Way (a.k.a. Hwy-103, the main road) and 45th Street. The Shelburne Inn also houses a friendly pub and a very good restaurant, **The Shoalwater,** rated among the best on the Washington coast. At the other end of the taste range, Long Beach is also the home of the 10-foot-tall "World's Largest Frying Pan," which hangs on a rack in front of the one-of-a-kind **Marsh's Free Museum** (360/642-2188), a totally tacky (and wonderfully kitsch) collection of postcards, peep shows, and old-time arcade games at 409 S. Pacific Way near 10th Street.

The rest of the slender Long Beach peninsula is quite quiet, dotted with cranberry bogs and historic fishing and oystering towns. In **Nahcotta,** a dozen miles north of Long Beach, you can stay overnight at the cozy **Moby Dick Hotel and Oyster Farm** ($75–120; 360/665-4543), at 25814 Sandridge Road, where they grow, harvest, and serve their own bivalve treats. Just north, **Oysterville** is the peninsula's oldest community, with some nifty historic homes dating back to the 1850s. The peninsula comes to an end in the north at **Leadbetter Point**

**State Park,** a great place for watching gulls, hawks, eagles, and migratory seabirds passing through on the Great Pacific Flyway.

For further information on the Long Beach Peninsula, contact the **visitors bureau** (360/642-2400) at the US-101/Hwy-103 junction.

## Cape Disappointment

The high headland marking the place where the Columbia River finally merges into the Pacific Ocean, **Cape Disappointment** was named by the early explorer Capt. John Meares, who in 1788 incorrectly interpreted the treacherous sandbars offshore to mean that, despite reports to the contrary, there was neither a major river nor any mythical Northwest Passage here.

Besides the grand view of the raging ocean, the best reason to visit the cape is to tour the small but worthwhile **Lewis and Clark Interpretive Center** (daily; $5; 360/642-3029), incongruously built atop a WW II–era artillery emplacement a short walk from the end of the road. On November 7, 1805, after five months and more than 4,000 miles, the explorers finally laid eyes on the Pacific from this point, then they sat through nine days of continuous rain before fleeing south to Oregon. Displays inside the museum give the overall context for their journey of discovery, walking you through the different stages of their two-year round-trip. The small "Cape D" lighthouse stands atop a 60-foot cliff, a half-mile walk from the Lewis and Clark museum. The more impressively photogenic North Head Lighthouse, on the ocean side of the peninsula a mile north of the museum, is the oldest on the West Coast.

A pair of statues sculpted by chain saws in a small state park, three miles west of the US-101 bridge across the Columbia River, marks the site where **Lewis and Clark** camped in December 1805 before heading south in search of better weather—which is about the only thing they never found on their epic trip.

The entire 2,000-acre area around the cape, including miles of beaches backed by rugged cliffs, is protected from development within **Cape Disappointment State Park** (360/642-3078), which has hiking, camping, and overnight lodgings in historic quarters next to North Head Lighthouse.

In recent years there have been a number of developments building on the area's Lewis and Clark connections, including an eight-mile "Discovery Trail" that heads north to the town of Long Beach, and a series of thought-provoking installations by architect Maya Lin (creator of the Washington, D.C. Vietnam Veterans Memorial). Called the Confluence Project, and located mostly along the riverfront east of the museum, these works all deal with the coming together of the natural and man-made worlds, as well as the interaction of explorers and Native Americans. The installations range from board-walks and interpretive trails (lined in places by quotations from Lewis and Clark's diaries), to a sculptural basalt "fish-cleaning" table.

The nearest services to Cape Disappointment—gas stations and a couple of cafés—are two miles away, back on US-101 in the rough-and-tumble fishing port of **Ilwaco.** Southeast of Ilwaco, toward the Oregon border, US-101 winds along the north bank of the Columbia River, giving good views of the mighty river's five-mile-wide mouth.

# OREGON

Rarely losing sight of the Pacific Ocean during its 365-mile jaunt along the Oregon coast, US-101 winds past rockbound coast, ancient forests, and innumerable towns and villages. While the region also has its share of strip towns and places where the timber boom went bust, the beach loops, historic restorations, and more state parks per mile than any place in the country soften its few hard edges. Every 20 miles or so, you'll pass through attractive, if moderately touristy, towns populated by at most a few thousand people, but as a general rule it's the mileage between these hamlets that explains why most people visit: to take in one of the most dramatic meetings of rock and tide in the world.

Starting in the north along the Columbia River at historic **Astoria,** one of the oldest settlements in the western United States, the route winds along the ocean past the very different beachfront hamlets of **Seaside** and **Cannon Beach**

By state law, there is no self-service gasoline in Oregon; all stations have attendants who pump the gas for you. There's no sales tax, either.

before edging slightly inland through the rich dairy lands of **Tillamook County.** Midway along, the popular vacation spots of **Lincoln City, Newport,** and **Florence** form the most developed corridor along the coast, but it's still easy to reach unpeopled stretches, especially at the remarkable **Oregon Dunes** stretching to the south. The dunes end abruptly at the heavily industrial port of **Coos Bay,** beyond which the natural beauty returns with a string of state parks and the diverse coastal towns of **Bandon, Port Orford, Gold Beach,** and **Brookings.**

## Astoria

The oldest American city west of the Missouri River, **Astoria** (pop. 9,813) is an upbeat mix of lovingly preserved past and busy contemporary commerce. Houses perched atop high hills overlook the Columbia River, creating a favorite backdrop for Hollywood movies. Despite its picturesque appearance, Astoria supports an active commercial fishing fleet and dozens of tugboats guide tankers and container ships across the treacherous sandbars. Founded by and named after fur-trade magnate John Jacob Astor in 1811, Astoria protected the tenuous American claim to the Pacific coast until the opening of the Oregon Trail brought substantial settlement. By the turn of the 20th century, Astoria was still Oregon's second-largest city, but the downturn in both salmon fishing and logging since the end of World War II has caused an economic decline which, as always, town officials look to tourism to overcome.

To find out about local issues and current events on the northern Oregon coast, pick up a copy of the excellent *Daily Astorian* newspaper, or tune to commercial-free **KMUN 91.5 FM** for NPR news and diverse programming.

US-101 crosses the Columbia River on the toll-free, high-level Astoria Bridge, completed in 1966, which drops you at the west end of the down-town waterfront. To get a sense of the lay of the land, follow the signs along 16th Street up Coxcomb Hill to the **Astoria Column** (daily 8 AM–dusk; $1) for a view of the Columbia meeting the

ocean, the coastal plain south to Tillamook Head, and the snowcapped Cascade Range (including, on a clear day, Mt. St. Helens) on the eastern horizon. A mosaic chronicling local history is wrapped like a ribbon around the column, tracing the many significant events in the town's past. A spiral staircase climbs to the top.

Back downtown at 441 8th Street, **Flavel House** (daily in summer; $5) is a red-roofed Queen Anne–style Victorian showplace restored as an elegantly furnished museum of Astoria's first millionaire, Columbia River pilot George Flavel. A half mile east, near the foot of 17th Street on the north side of waterfront Marine Drive, the **Columbia River Maritime Museum** (daily; $8; 503/325-2323) displays a large and very impressive collection that tells the story of the lifeblood of this community: the Columbia River.

Fortify yourself at one of the many good seafood places along the water, starting at the funky, ever-popular **Columbian Café,** 1114 Marine Drive (503/325-2233), where chef Uriah Hulsey prepares all sorts of ultra-fresh food in an impossibly cramped galley kitchen. Meals are massive yet reasonably priced, so be sure to arrive with an appetite; breakfast and lunch are served daily, dinner Wednesday–Saturday. Another Astoria eating option is the casual **Ship Inn** (503/325-0033), serving halibut fish-and-chips under the bridge at Marine Drive and 2nd Street, while foodies might want to visit adjacent **Josephson's Smokehouse** (503/325-2190), at 106 Marine Drive, to sample the delicious array of smoked salmon, which is prepared on the premises and sold all over the country.

To absorb a full portion of Astoria's addictive ambience, stay the night at the riverview **Crest Motel** ($70 and up; 503/325-3141), three miles east of town along US-30 at 5366 Leif Erickson Drive, or in town at the luxurious and historic

**Hotel Elliott,** 357 12th Street ($140 and up; 503/325-2222). Astoria also has a handful of nice B&Bs like the 1890s **Astoria Inn** ($80 and up; 503/325-8153), at 3391 Irving Avenue. For detailed listings or further information, contact the **Astoria Chamber of Commerce** (503/325-6311), located at 111 W. Marine Drive.

## Fort Clatsop

In the conifer forests six miles south of Astoria and three miles east of US-101, the **Fort Clatsop National Memorial** (daily; $5 per car; 503/861-2471) is a credible reconstruction of the encampment Lewis and Clark and company constructed during the winter of 1805–1806. Now the centerpiece of the sprawling, multi-state Lewis and Clark National Historical Park, Fort Clatsop has been fully (and in many ways more accurately) rebuilt after a 2005 fire destroyed the first (circa 1955) replica. The fort itself is joined by a range of exhibits in the visitors center, a quarter mile away. A longer (eight-mile round-trip) trail leads to the coast, and summertime living history reenactments help conjure the travails of two centuries ago. The expedition spent three miserable months here, mingling occasionally with the native Clatsop and Chinook tribes but mostly growing moldy in the incessant rain and damp while being bitten by fleas, sewing new moccasins, and making salt in preparation for the return journey across the continent.

**Fort Stevens,** off US-101 on the way to Fort Clatsop, was the only continental U.S. fortification bombed during WW II, sustaining a shelling from a Japanese submarine on June 21, 1942.

## Gearhart

In between burly Astoria and the boisterous beach resort of Seaside, but a world away from its neighbors in terms of character and ambience, the tiny town of **Gearhart** (pop. 995) was the sometime home of influential chef and cookbook author James Beard. Beard's culinary legacy lives on in the **Pacific Way Bakery and Cafe** (503/738-0245), a half mile west of US-101

the end of the Lewis and Clark Trail

at 601 Pacific Way, which offers the coast's best coffees and crois-
sants, along with four-star lunches and dinners. Like many places
along the Oregon coast, it's closed Tuesday and Wednesday.

## Seaside

Nothing along the Oregon coast prepares you for the carnival
ambience of downtown **Seaside** (pop. 5,900), Oregon's oldest
seafront resort. Ben Holladay, who built the place in 1873, included a racetrack, zoo, and plush hotel to lure Portlanders to
ride his rail line to the beach. Come during spring break, or
on a weekend during July or August, and join the 50,000 or
more visitors wandering among th e saltwater-taffy stands and
video-game arcades along Broadway, or cruising the concrete
boardwalk (called The Prom) along the beach.

Where Broadway meets the beach, a small traffic circle
known locally as The Turnaround is marked by a statue and a
sign proclaiming the town The End of the Lewis and Clark
Trail. South of here, between Beach Drive and The Prom, is a
replica of the Lewis and Clark **salt cairn,** where the explorers
boiled seawater nonstop for seven weeks to produce enough
salt to preserve meat for their return trip east. From the south
end of Seaside, you can follow a challenging but very reward-
ing five-mile trail over Tillamook Head to Ecola State Park.

A half mile north of downtown, housed in a wood-shin-
gled old motor court on the banks of the Necanicum River,
the **Seaside International Hostel** (503/738-7911), at 930
Holladay Drive, has dorm beds, private rooms, canoes and
kayaks, an espresso bar, and nightly movies. There are dozens of motels and a handful of B&Bs in Seaside, booked
solid in summer and serene, verging on lonely, come wintertime. For listings and other information, contact the **Seaside
Visitors Bureau** (503/738-3097 or 888/306-2326), at 7 N.
Roosevelt Drive.

## Ecola State Park

Just north of Cannon Beach, a mile south of the junction between US-101 and US-26 from Portland, the rainforested access road through **Ecola State Park** (day use only; $3 per car;
503/436-2844) leads you to one of the most photographed
views on the coast: Looking south you can see Haystack Rock
and Cannon Beach with Neahkahnie Mountain looming
above them. Out to sea, the sight of **Tillamook Rock
Lighthouse** to the northwest is also striking. Operational

# Portland

Portland, Oregon's largest city, is located inland from the coast near the confluence of the Willamette and Columbia Rivers. Due to its strategic location, the pioneer municipality grew so fast it was nicknamed Stumptown for the hundreds of fir stumps left by early loggers, and while railroad tracks and other heavy industrial remnants are still highly visible around town, Portland's riverfront park and numerous winding greenways show that this mini metropolis is not a smokestack town but a community that values art and nature as highly as commerce. Along with the largest (5,000-acre Forest Park) and the smallest (24-inches-in-diameter Mill Ends Park) urban parks in the nation, and one of the coolest urban skate parks anywhere (under the Burnside Bridge), Portland also has more movie theaters, restaurants, microbreweries, and bookstores per capita than any other U.S. city.

The oldest part of Portland has, over the past few years, been renovated into a lively Old Town district, where cast-iron facades of 120-year-old buildings hold some of the city's most popular bars, clubs, and cafés. (Not to mention general weirdness magnets like the 24-Hour Church of Elvis, most recently found at 408 N.W. Couch Street.) South of Old Town along the river, an ugly freeway has been torn down to form the mile-long Tom McCall Waterfront Park, and west of the river, downtown Portland centers on lively Pioneer Courthouse Square, at 6th Avenue and Yamhill Street. South of the square, the South Park Blocks between Park and Ninth Avenues were set aside as parklands in the original city plan and are now bounded by Portland's prime museums. One essential Portland place is north of the square: **Powell's Books** (503/228-0540), at 1005 W. Burnside Street across from the Blitz-Weinhard Brewery, is the largest (and certainly among the best) new-and-used bookshop in the world.

One of the largest and oldest ballparks in the minor leagues, the circa-1926 Civic Stadium, downtown off Burnside at 1844 SW Morrison, has been fully renovated and redubbed PGE Park, home to the **Portland Beavers** (503/553-5555), the San Diego Padres' top farm club.

Along the river south of town, **Oaks Park** (503/233-5777) is a wonderful circa-1905 amusement park, with ancient and modern thrill rides all packed together in a sylvan, oak tree–dotted park.

## Practicalities

Air travelers can land at Portland International Airport (PDX), but most long-distance flights here come and go via Seattle's Sea-Tac, which is only about 2.5 hours' drive north, via the I-5 freeway. Getting around public-spirited Portland is a breeze thanks to the combination of an efficient bus system and a light rail train (called MAX; 503/238-7433).

Though it doesn't have a trendy reputation, Portland does have some great restaurants in all stripes and sizes. **Esparza's Tex-Mex,** 2725 SE Ankeny Street (503/234-7909), hidden away behind a hole-in-the-wall facade a block south of E. Burnside Street, is worth searching out for its smoky pork tacos and a jukebox featuring Tejano, norteño, and Marty Robbins hits. For more traditional Portland fare, head to **Jake's Famous Crawfish** (503/226-1419), at 401 SW 12th Street, which for over a century has been the place to go for the finest, freshest seafood. For meat, nothing beats the **Ringside** (503/223-1513), near PGE Park at 2165 W. Burnside Street, long famous for its great beef, fine fried chicken, monster Walla Walla sweet onion rings, and Hemingway-esque ambience. If your taste happens to run more to Marilyn Manson than Marilyn Monroe, you'll probably prefer to eat across town at **Dots Cafe** (503/235-0203), at 2521 SE Clinton Street, a late-night hangout that has comfy dark booths, great black-bean burritos, micro-brews, and pool tables.

VIEW FROM A SKYLINER, PORTLAND, OREGON, MT. HOOD IN THE DISTANCE

There are all sorts of places to stay in Portland, starting with a pair of popular **HI-Portland Hostels,** one east of downtown at 3031 Hawthorne Boulevard (503/236-3380) and a newer one in the Northwest District, at 425 NW 18th Avenue (503/241-2783). The stylish, comfortable, and close-to-downtown **Hotel DeLuxe** ($150 and up; 503/219-2094) is a newly renovated boutique hotel at 729 SW 15th Avenue. If you feel like splurging, try another impeccably restored downtown landmark, the **Heathman Hotel** ($199 and up; 503/241-4100 or 800/551-0011), at 1009 SW Broadway, with an elegant lobby and sumptuously appointed (if somewhat small) rooms.

The best source of visitor information on Portland is the **Portland Visitors Association** (503/275-9750 or 800/962-3700), on Pioneer Courthouse Square.

Heathman Hotel

from 1881 to 1957, the lighthouse is now used as a repository for the ashes of people who've been cremated.

The rest of Ecola State Park protects a series of rugged headlands stretching for nine miles along the coast, with many forested hiking trails including some of the most scenic portions of the Oregon Coast Trail System. The park also marks the southernmost extent of Lewis and Clark's cross-country expedition. Clark and a few other members of the Corps of Discovery expedition traversed the area in search of supplements to their diet of hardtack and dried salmon. The word "ecola" means whale in the Chinookan tongue and was affixed to this region by the Lewis and Clark expedition, who found one of these leviathans washed up on a beach. They happily bought 300 pounds of tangy whale blubber from local Indians, but these days you'd better bring your own lunch to picnic atop bluffs with sweeping views of the rock-strewn Pacific. The view from the top of **Tillamook Head,** which rises 1,200 feet above the sea at the heart of the park, was memorialized by explorer William Clark as "the grandest and most pleasing prospect" he had ever beheld.

## Cannon Beach

Unlike many Oregon coast towns, **Cannon Beach** (pop. 1,588) is hidden from the highway, but it's one place you won't want to miss. Though it's little more than a stone's throw south of boisterous Seaside, Cannon Beach has long been known as an artists' colony, and while it has grown considerably in recent years thanks to its popularity as a weekend escape from Portland, it retains a peaceful, rustic atmosphere.

At the start of summer, Cannon Beach hosts the largest and most enjoyable **sand castle competition** on the West Coast, with some 10,000 spectators and as many as 1,000 participants turning out with their buckets and spades. In terms of traditional "tourist attractions," there's not a lot to do, but Cannon Beach is an unbeatable place in which to stop and unwind, or to take long walks along the seven-mile strand and then retreat indoors to the many good galleries,

Haystack Rock

cafés, and restaurants. For breakfast or brunch, fill up on eggs Benedict at the **Lazy Susan Cafe** (closed Tues. and Wed. in winter; 503/436-2816), at 126 N. Hemlock Street; it also serves a stupendous array of ice cream at its "scoop shop" up the street. Another great, casual gourmet place to eat is **Ecola Seafoods,** 208 N. Spruce Street (503/436-9130), which serves locally caught fish and shellfish—including an excellent $5 chowder.

Reasonably priced rooms near the beach and town can be found at the **McBee Motel Cottages** ($69–129; 503/436-2569), at 888 S. Hemlock Street. There are also many nice, quaint B&Bs around Cannon Beach, like the oceanfront **Sea Sprite,** 280 Nebesna Street ($140 and up; 503/436-2266).

South of Cannon Beach, the Beach Loop, an extension of Hemlock, runs along a spectacular grouping of volcanic plugs, notably 235-foot-high **Haystack Rock.**

## Neahkahnie Mountain and Oswald West State Park

South of Cannon Beach, US-101 rises high above the Pacific. Nowhere else along the Oregon coast does the roadbed offer such a sweeping ocean view. Soaring another thousand feet above the highway is **Neahkahnie Mountain,** which offers unsurpassed views up and down the coast. About 10 miles south of Cannon Beach at **Oswald West State Park** (503/368-3575), a half-mile trail winds beneath the highway through an ancient forest to driftwood-laden (and surfer-friendly) Short Sands Beach and the tidepools of Smuggler's Cove. Named for an early Governor of Oregon who successfully proposed preserving and protecting the beaches of Oregon as state (rather than private) property, Oswald West State Park is a good start for longer hikes, to weather-beaten Cape Falcon or across US-101 to the summit of Neahkahnie Mountain.

South of Neahkahnie Mountain, and thus spared much of the stormy coastal weather (annual rainfall hereabouts averages 80 inches), is the upscale resort town of **Manzanita.** Nearby **Nehalem Bay State Park** (503/368-5154) has a large campground with hundreds of sites and plenty of hot showers. US-101 continues through a series of small towns before winding inland past the sloughs and dairy country along Tillamook Bay.

## Tillamook

With cows outnumbering people by more than two to one, **Tillamook** (pop. 4,352) sprawls over lush grasslands at the

Tillamook Cheese Factory

southern end of Tillamook Bay. Its motto, "Cheese, trees, and ocean breeze," conjures a clear sense of a place where the high school football team is cheered on by shouts of "Go Cheesemakers!" Tillamook (a Salish word meaning land of many waters) is dominated by the **Tillamook Cheese Factory** at the north end of town, one of the busiest tourist draws in the state. Inside, a self-guided tour with informational placards traces Tillamook cheese-making from the last century to the present, and a glassed-in observation area lets you watch the stuff being made and packaged.

Tillamook's other odd attraction is east of US-101 and south of town. One of the world's largest wooden structures—300 feet wide, 1,100 feet long, and nearly 200 feet tall, enclosing six acres of open-span floor space—has been preserved as the **Tillamook Air Museum** (daily; $9.50 adults; 503/842-1130). Built in 1942, the structure is now a museum telling the story of the WW II surveillance blimps kept here by the U.S. Navy. There are also displays about other dirigible craft (like the ill-fated Hindenburg) as well as a world-class collection of vintage airplanes (from MiG fighters to an elegant, twin-tailed P-38 Lightning), plus a theater and a restaurant, all making for a fascinating and unusual stop. The building used to be one of a pair of hangars, but the other one burned down in 1992.

## Three Capes Loop

US-101 veers inland for 50 miles between Tillamook and Lincoln City, the next sizable town south. If time and weather are on your side, head west along the coast via the well-signed, 35-mile-long **Three Capes Loop.** Running northwest from Tillamook, the loop reaches the mouth of Tillamook Bay at **Cape Meares,** which has a restored 1890 lighthouse and an oddly contorted Sitka spruce known as the Octopus Tree.

Heading south through the coastal villages of **Oceanside** and **Netarts,** the loop proceeds through dairy country until it climbs onto the shoulder of **Cape Lookout,** where a small sign proclaiming Wildlife Viewing Area marks the beginning

Seven miles south of Tillamook, a turnoff east follows a bumpy, one-mile access road leading to the highest waterfall in Oregon's Coast Range, 266-foot **Munson Creek Falls.** From the parking area at the end of the road, a short trail leads to this year-round cascade.

of a 2.5-mile trail that leads through an ancient forest to the tip of the cape, 100-plus feet above the water. Besides the coastal panorama, in winter and spring this is a prime place to view passing gray whales. From the trailhead, the middle path leads to the cape, while others to the left and right lead down to the water. **Cape Lookout State Park** (503/842-4981) has the area's most popular campground, where tent sites, yurts, and cabins come with hot showers and other creature comforts.

The Oregon coast's most famous promontory, **Cape Kiwanda,** sees some of the state's wildest surf battering the sandstone headland. Across from the cape is **Haystack Rock,** a 327-foot sea stack a half mile offshore. Along the beach south of the cape, surfers ride waves while fisherfolk skid their small dories along the sands every afternoon—a sight worth hanging around to see.

The southernmost settlement on this scenic alternative to US-101 is neighboring **Pacific City,** where two great places to eat, the **Grateful Bread Bakery** (503/965-7337) and **The Riverhouse** (503/965-6722), sit beachside on Brooten Road.

## Lincoln City

The most developed section of the Oregon coast stretches for miles along US-101 through **Lincoln City** (pop. 7,437), seven miles of strip malls, outlet stores, fast-food franchises, and motels. With more than 1,000 oceanside rooms, Lincoln City does offer some of the coast's cheapest lodging, especially in the off-season when sign after sign advertises rooms for as low as $35 a night. But apart from inexpensive accommodations, with so much scenic splendor nearby there's no great reason to linger.

The one great man-made attraction hereabouts is five miles northeast of Lincoln City, just east of US-101 on Hwy-18, the main road to and from Portland: the **Otis Café,** 1259 Salmon River Highway (541/994-2813), which immortalizes American road food, offering excellent waffles and other breakfast treats along with epicurean lunches and fresh berry pies for dessert. The Otis Café is open for breakfast and lunch daily, plus dinner Thursday–Sunday.

Seven miles south of Lincoln City, a sign announces the

**Salishan Lodge** (541/764-3600), a beautifully landscaped rustic resort with a five-star dining room and a surprisingly affordable coffee shop, **The Sun Room.** Down the hill across US-101, **Siletz Bay** is a bird-watcher's paradise, where hawks and herons and thousands of other seabirds (along with chinook salmon and cutthroat trout) are protected within a federal wildlife refuge.

## Depoe Bay

Depoe Bay has an appeal, but so much of its natural beauty is obscured from the highway by gift shops or intruded upon by traffic that you've got to know where to look. In his book *Blue Highways,* William Least Heat-Moon wrote "Depoe Bay used to be a picturesque fishing village; now it was just picturesque." While it's true that most of the commercial fishing is long gone, you can still park your car along the highway and walk out on the bridge to watch sportfishing boats move through the narrow channel to what the *Guinness Book of World Records* rates as the world's smallest navigable harbor. South of the bridge is another record-setter, the Oregon coast's largest secondhand bookstore, the **Channel Bookstore** (541/765-2352).

> Depoe Bay was originally known as Depot Bay, named after a local Siletz Indian who worked at the local U.S. Army depot and called himself **Charlie Depot.**

The **Sea Hag** restaurant (541/765-2734), on US-101 in downtown Depoe Bay, is a time-tested breakfast place, and people drive for miles to enjoy the pies at the **Spouting Horn,** overlooking the harbor. For a place to stay, try the **Inn at Arch Rock,** 70 NW Sunset Street ($120 and up; 800/767-1835).

## Cape Foulweather and the Devil's Punchbowl

Between Depoe Bay and Newport, the roadside scenery along US-101 and the parallel "old road," now signed as the Otter Crest Loop, is dominated by miles of broad beaches and sandstone bluffs, including the 453-foot headland of **Cape Foulweather,** named by Capt. James Cook and offering a 360-degree coastal panorama. The Otter Crest Loop has frequently been closed by slides and reconstruction efforts, but you can reach it from many access roads. With fine old bridges and numerous vistas, it's a great drive—or bicycle route.

Farther south, midway between Depoe Bay and Newport, the aptly named **Devil's Punchbowl** gives a ringside seat on a frothy confrontation between rock and tide. In the parking area you'll find a small lunch café (a branch of Newport's **Mo's**) graced by a chair where "The Boss" (singer Bruce Springsteen) sat on June 11, 1987.

## Newport

Another old fishing community turned tourist nexus, **Newport** (pop. 9,532) started in the 1860s on the strength of sweet-tasting Yaquina Bay oysters, which were in demand from San Francisco to New York City and are still available at local restaurants. Oysters, crabs, and clams, along with sea otters, sea lions, sharks, and seabirds, are the stars of the show at the large and modern **Oregon Coast Aquarium** (daily; $14; 541/867-3474), south of Newport across the Yaquina Bay Bridge. The aquarium includes an aquatic aviary, where sea lions, tufted puffins, and other shorebirds cavort in a simulated rockbound coastal habitat, and over 40,000 square feet of similarly eco-friendly exhibits, much of it outdoors.

On the north side of the US-101 bridge over Yaquina

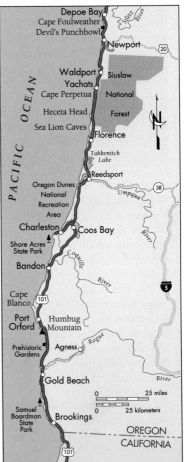

Bay, turn onto Hubert Street and head for the bayfront, where boatyards and fish-packing plants service a working harbor. Though it's still the state's second-largest fishing port, much of Newport's bayfront has been consumed by souvenir shops, a wax museum, a Ripley's Believe It or Not, and other tourist traps. But you'll find the original **Mo's,** a locally famous seafood restaurant, at 622 Bay Boulevard (541/265-2979).

The coast and inland forests along the Siletz River near Depoe Bay and Newport were the primary location of the **Ken Kesey** novels and films *One Flew Over the Cuckoo's Nest* and *Sometimes a Great Notion.*

North of the harbor is **Nye Beach,** an interesting mélange of old-fashioned beach houses and destination resorts on the western side of US-101. **Don Petrie's** (541/265-3663) serves excellent Italian food at 613 NW 3rd Street. Nye Beach is also home to hotels, motels, and the bohemian **Sylvia Beach Hotel,** 267 NW Cliff Street ($120–up; 541/265-5428), *the* place to stay in Newport for anyone of literary bent. If you can't afford the private rooms—with decor evocative of different authors, including a scary Edgar Allan Poe room based on "The Pit and the Pendulum"—there are dormitory bunk beds for around $25 a night. All rates include breakfast.

The old-growth forests of the **Drift Creek Wilderness** east of Waldport are prime nesting areas for the endangered northern spotted owl, whose numbers are still declining.

## Waldport

If you want to avoid lines and general tourist bustle, **Waldport** is a nice alternative to the resort towns surrounding it. Tourism is low-key here, and you can still sense the vestiges of the resource-based economy, a by-product of the town's proximity to rich timber stands and superlative fishing. Stop along US-101 at the **Alsea Bay Bridge Interpretive Center** (541/563-2002) for interesting exhibits on coastal transportation and the local Alsea tribe, as well as a telescope trained on waterfowl and seals in the bay. The center sits at the south foot of the modern span that, in 1991, replaced the historic (circa-1936) art deco–style bridge. From the north end of the bridge, you can follow Hwy-34 seven miles upstream to the **Kozy Kove Kafe** (541/528-3251), a floating restaurant with good food and bucolic riverside ambience.

A little more than two miles south of Waldport, **Cape Cod Cottages** ($65–125; 541/563-2106), at 4150 US-101, is a good choice for location and comfort. Four miles south of

Waldport, halfway to Yachats, **Beachside State Recreation Area** (541/563-3220) has a very popular campground, with hot showers, RV hookups, even a coin laundry. And there's a lovely stretch of sandy beach.

## Yachats

On the way into **Yachats** (pop. 617; pronounced YA-hots), beach loops on either side of the Yachats River give a sense of why the area is called "the gem of the Oregon coast." It's a great place to wander and get lost and found again, especially at the beautiful **Ocean Road State Natural Area,** where incredible views along a one-mile loop road look out over crashing waves, tidepools, blowholes, and, in winter, gray whales migrating offshore.

Back in town, for the past 30-plus years, **Leroy's Blue Whale** (541/547-3399), on US-101 at 580 Coast Highway, has been serving breakfast, lunch, and dinner every day, featuring fluffy pancakes, fresh chowders, and fine fish-and-chips.

The word "cottage" is a popular lodging label around Yachats, usually referring to a moderately priced, self-contained cabin or duplex with kitchen. On US-101 there are a half dozen different cottage complexes, each fronting the beach. If you want more than a simple place to spend the night, the **Oregon House** ($95 and up; 541/547-3329) on US-101 nine miles south of Yachats has spacious apartment-like rooms, some with fireplaces and ocean views, and all with access to the well-tended grounds and trails leading down the bluffs to a gem of a sandy cove.

## Cape Perpetua

For nearly 400 miles along the Oregon coast, US-101 abounds with national forests, state parks, and viewpoints. But unless you have your whole lifetime to spend here, **Cape Perpetua,** two miles south of Yachats, deserves most of your attention. Stop first at the **Siuslaw National Forest visitors center** (541/547-3289), just east of US-101, for seacoast views and exhibits on forestry and area history. From the visitors center, trails lead across the highway past wind-bent trees, piles of seashells and other artifacts left behind by native peoples, excellent tidepools, and two rock formations, Spouting Horn and the Devil's Churn. During stormy seas, both shoot huge spouts of foam into the air. The friendly folks at the visitors center can also point you toward Cape Perpetua's small, summer-only campground, which has bathrooms but no showers or hookups.

You can reach the top of 800-foot-high Cape Perpetua itself by following a two-mile-long road, marked by Cape Perpetua Viewpoint signs and leaving US-101 100 yards or so north of the visitors center. Once atop the cape, walk the **Trail of the Whispering Spruce,** a half-mile loop around the rim of the promontory that yields, on a clear day, 150-mile views of the Oregon coast from a rustic, WPA-built stone observation point.

## Heceta Head and the Sea Lion Caves

Halfway between Cape Perpetua and Florence, a small bridge just south of Carl Washburne State Park marks the turnoff to **Heceta Head Lighthouse,** perhaps the most photographed beacon in the United States. Built in 1893, it was named for the Spanish mariner who is credited with being the first European to set foot in the region. You'll have to be content with gazing at it across the cove from a small but rarely crowded beach, unless you stay at the quaint old lighthouse keeper's quarters, restored as an unforgettable B&B ($150 and up; 541/547-3696).

Farther along US-101, 10 miles north of Florence, traffic slows to a stop at the gift shop that serves as the entrance to **Sea Lion Caves** (daily; $10). You can ride an elevator down to America's largest sea cave, the only mainland rookery for the Steller sea lion. Fall and winter offer the best times to see (and smell!) these animals, which throng together here during mating season. When the weather's nice, you can often watch them swimming in the ocean (for free, without the seal smells . . . ) from a viewpoint 100 yards up US-101.

## Florence

If first and last impressions are enduring, **Florence** is truly blessed. As you enter the city from the north, US-101 climbs high above the ocean; coming from the south, travelers are greeted by the graceful **Siuslaw River Bridge,** perhaps the most impressive of a half dozen WPA-built spans designed by Conde McCullough and decorated with his trademark Egyptian obelisks and art deco stylings. Unfortunately, first impressions feel a little misleading, since much of what you can see from US-101 is a bland highway sprawl of motels, gas stations, and franchised restaurants.

The best part of Florence, **Old Town,** is just upstream from that landmark bridge, along the north bank of the Siuslaw River. Here, among Bay Street's three blocks of interesting boutiques and galleries, you'll find a number of cafés and seafood restaurants. Old Town Florence is also home to the very welcoming **Edwin K. B&B** ($100–150; 541/997-8360) at 1155 Bay Street, a lovely white Craftsman-style home built in 1914 by one of the town's founders.

Back along US-101, car culture fans will relish the chance to eat burgers and fries at **Bliss' Hot Rod Grill,** 1179 US-101 (541/997-6726), where walls are covered in old road signs and some of the spacious booths are made from classic 1950s American cars.

## "Dune Country": Oregon's Sahara

For nearly 50 miles south of Florence, US-101 has an extensive panorama of oceanfront dunes. Though the dunes are often obscured from view by forests, roadside signs indicate access roads to numerous dunescapes on both sides of the highway. Coming from the north, the first of these access points is **Honeyman State Park,** 10 miles south of Florence, where rhododendrons line a half-mile trail leading to a 150-foot-high dune overlooking a mirage-like lake.

Giant rhododendrons and tumble-down shacks that rent out dune buggies and ATVs line US-101 between Florence and Coos Bay. One of the best of these rental places is **Sandland Adventures** (541/997-8087), a mile south of Florence's Siuslaw River bridge, which also offers thrilling, sand-in-your-mouth guided dune buggy tours.

Before setting out on any extended exploration, your first stop should be the USFS-run **Oregon Dunes visitors center** (541/271-3611) at the junction of US-101 and Hwy-38 in **Reedsport,** along the Umpqua River midway between Florence and Coos Bay at the heart of the dunes. The helpful rangers can provide detailed information on hiking and camping throughout the park. Reedsport itself has a line of motels and burger joints—**Don's Diner,** on US-101 at 2115 Winchester Avenue (541/271-2032), has legions of fans. You'll find one more interesting option just north of Reedsport in the **Gardiner Guest House** (541/271-

Fans of **Frank Herbert's** ecological sci-fi saga **Dune** may already know that the stories were inspired by the Oregon Dunes, south of Florence.

4005), which offers comfortable B&B rooms in a restored Victorian home at 401 Front Street.

Perhaps the best introduction to the bewildering geography of the dunes region is Umpqua Dunes, nine miles south of the Reedsport visitors center. Another popular walk starts from Eel Creek Campground, heading for just under two miles across small marshes and conifer groves en route to the sea, negotiating lunar-like dunes soaring 300–500 feet—some of the tallest in the world. Another nice trek leaves from Tahkenitch Lake, a popular freshwater bass fishing spot north of Gardiner, and gives a more in-depth look at the dunes' diverse flora and fauna, including swans and (very rarely!) black bears.

## Coos Bay

Even if you race right through, it's quite apparent that **Coos Bay** (pop. 15,374), once the world's largest lumber port, retains a core of heavy industry. Though many of the big mills have closed, you can still watch huge piles of wood chips, the harbor's number-one export, being loaded onto factory ships in the harbor east of US-101. The chips are sent to Asia, where they're turned into paper. (One chip-ship that didn't make it into

Behind the Coos Bay visitors bureau, a monument remembers the region's favorite son, middle-distance runner **Steve Prefontaine,** who electrified the athletic world before his death in a 1974 car wreck, at the age of 24. An annual 10K memorial run is held every September.

the harbor, the 700-foot-long *New Carissa,* wrecked in a 1999 storm and sat on the Coos Bay beach for years.)

Big breakfasts, eclectic but inexpensive lunches and dinners, great pies, and a good range of microbrews are served at the **Blue Heron** (541/267-3933), at 100 Commercial Avenue, across from the visitors bureau. There's no shortage of easy-to-find lodging, including **Motel 6** ($45–65; 541/267-7171) on US-101 at 1445 N. Bayshore.

## Shore Acres State Park

The historical antecedents for Coos Bay port development were laid a century ago by the Simpson Lumber Company, whose ships transported Oregon logs around the world. The ships returned with seeds that were planted in the Simpson estate's garden, 12 miles west of Coos Bay via the Cape Arago Highway, three miles beyond the busy commercial and sportfishing port of Charleston. Though the Simpson house burned to the ground in 1923, the 750-acre gardens are still a floral fantasia, now open to the public as **Shore Acres State Park** (daily 9 AM–dusk). Besides the formal gardens, which are illuminated during the Christmas holiday season, there's an observation tower above wave-battered bluffs and a trail down to a delightful beach.

On the way to Shore Acres from Coos Bay is **Sunset Bay State Park,** perhaps Oregon's best swimming beach. South of Shore Acres is **Cape Arago State Park,** complete with tidepools and seals on offshore rocks.

## Bandon

There's no sharper contrast on the Oregon coast than the difference between industrial Coos Bay and earthy **Bandon** (pop. 2,833), 23 miles to the south. Here, in the **Old Town** section along the

banks of the Coquille River, are several blocks of galleries, crafts shops, and fine restaurants, marked by a gateway arch off US-101. Start a tour of Old Town at the corner of 1st and Baltimore, where Big Wheel Farm Supply houses the **Bandon Driftwood Museum** (daily; free). The combination of sculpted tree roots and fertilizer displays gives a good sense of Bandon's back-to-the-land, hippie ethos. A more academic introduction to the

Bandon Lighthouse

town and region can be had at the new and improved **Coquille River Museum** (Mon.–Sat., daily in summer; $2; 541/347-2164), at 270 Fillmore Street. Its exhibits on area history, cranberries, and local color are artfully done, and the building on US-101 is easy to find, so be sure to stop. South of town from 1st Street, a **Beach Loop** runs along a ridge overlooking a fantastic assemblage of coastal monoliths.

For fish-and-chips along the waterfront, the **Bandon Fish Market,** 249 1st Street (541/347-4282), is cheap and cheerful; for sit-down fare and a view of the lighthouse, head to **Bandon Boatworks,** 275 SW Lincoln Avenue (541/347-2111).

Outside of town, the exclusive and expensive (but open to the public) **Bandon Dunes Golf Resort** ($500 and up; 541/347-4380 or 888/345-6008) has been drawing raves from golfers, well-heeled vacationers, and landscape architects alike. Designed to preserve and enhance the "natural" scenery in the style of Scottish "links" courses rather than the anodyne green swaths that characterize most suburban country club courses, Bandon Dunes offers golf (at $250 per round!), select accommodations, and a nice restaurant.

South of Bandon, 11 miles north of Port Orford, **Cape Blanco** is considered—by Oregonians, at least—the westernmost point of land in the contiguous United States. Named by early Spanish explorers for the white shells encrusting the 245-foot cliff face, the cape is also the site of Oregon's oldest (circa-1870) and highest lighthouse. The headland offers great views, and its windswept exposure draws pilots of radio-controlled model planes and gliders. If you need to warm your innards afterwards, stop in at the straightforward **Greasy Spoon Café** (541/348-2514) on US-101 in nearby Langlois for a cup of coffee and some classic biscuits-and-gravy.

## Port Orford and Humbug Mountain

Pastoral sheep ranches, cranberry bogs, berry fields, and Christmas tree farms dominate the 25-mile stretch south of Bandon, but as you pull into **Port Orford** (pop. 1,025), you can't help but notice a huge volcanic plug abutting the crescent-shaped shoreline. Known as **Battle Rock,** in memory of a battle (re-enacted every 4th of July) in which early settlers fought off a party of hostile Indians, the rock is impressive from the harbor below, while a trail climbs up to the wind-blown summit. Due to the southwest orientation, which subjects the harbor to turbulent winds and constant waves, fishing boats have to be lowered into the water by crane, but surfers (and kite-surfers and windsurfers) don't seem to mind.

People who keep track of these things say that tiny **Port Orford** is the "Most Westerly Incorporated City in the Continental United States." Others grant it the less-welcome title of "rainiest place on the Oregon coast."

A nice place to stay in Port Orford is the **Home by the Sea B&B** ($90–120; 541/332-2855 or 877/332-2855), at 444 Jackson Street, within walking distance to town along yet another stunning stretch of Oregon coastline.

Six miles south of Port Orford you'll come to **Humbug Mountain,** whose 1,756-foot elevation flanks the west side of the highway. It's the coast's highest peak rising directly off the beach, and its steep contours and tree-covered slopes are best appreciated from the steep but well-maintained three-mile trail that climbs to the summit. The mountain's name was bestowed by prospectors who found that tales of gold deposits here were just "humbug," but the views from the top are splendid.

## Prehistoric Gardens

On the west side of the highway, midway between Port Orford and Gold Beach, you'll come across one of the Oregon coast's tackiest but most enduring and enjoyable tourist traps, the **Prehistoric Gardens** (daily; $8 adults; 541/332-4463). Standing out like a sore thumb on this otherwise unspoiled stretch of US-101, a collection of brightly colored, more or less life-sized dinosaur sculptures inhabits the evocatively lush green forest. Since 1953, when amateur paleontologist E. V. Nelson sculpted his first concrete *T. rex,* two dozen more have been added to the forest menagerie.

Southern Oregon's coastal forests yield the increasingly rare and disease-threatened **Port Orford cedar,** a very valuable (up to $50,000 per tree) and very fragrant wood popular for use in Japanese home construction.

Mt. Emily, just east of Brookings, was bombed by a submarine-launched Japanese seaplane in September 1942. Though the Japanese plans to ignite the entire coastline in a massive forest fire fizzled, the attack weakened a short-lived secession movement by southern Oregonians and Northern Californians to establish a new state called **Jefferson.**

## Gold Beach

**Gold Beach** was named for the nuggets mined from the area's black sands during the mid-19th century, but despite its name this is one coastal town where the action is definitely *away* from the beach. The **Rogue River** defines the northern city limits and is the town's economic raison d'être. During salmon season, Gold Beach hotels and restaurants fill up with anglers, while **jet-boat tours** of the wild river are also a draw. Along with many other operators hawking their services with billboards next to the highway, **Jerry's Rogue Jets** ($42 and up;

541/247-4571 or 800/451-3645), by the bridge at the north end of town, takes passengers upstream to the isolated hamlet of **Agness,** where a homespun mountain lodge serves family-style fried-chicken lunches and dinners (the food is not included in the price of the jet-boat ride). Other trips head farther upstream to the Rogue River rapids and the roadless wilderness areas of the **Siskiyou National Forest;** these cost $50–75.

The usual motel rooms are available along US-101, but for a more memorable visit, try the **Tu Tu Tun Lodge,** 96550 North Bank Rogue ($90 and up; 541/247-6664 or 800/864-6357). Set on a hill above the Rogue River, seven miles upstream from the coast, this upscale fishing lodge (pronounced ta-TWO-tun) has plushly rustic rooms and a great restaurant.

## Samuel Boardman State Park

Between Gold Beach and Brookings, US-101's windy, hilly roadbed is studded with the cliffside ocean vistas, giant conifers, and boomerang-shaped offshore rock formations of **Samuel Boardman State Park.** The park covers most of the "Fabulous 50" miles between the two towns, and all of the above-mentioned features come together at Natural Bridges Cove. Located just north of the Thomas Creek Bridge (the highest bridge on the coast north of San Francisco's Golden Gate), this turnout is easy to miss despite being well signed because, from the highway, it appears to be simply a parking lot fronting some trees. From the south end of the parking lot, however, a short trail through an old-growth forest leads to a viewpoint several hundred feet above three natural rock archways standing out from an azure cove.

## Brookings: Harris Beach State Park

The drive through the malled-over main drag of **Brookings** offers only fleeting glimpses of the Pacific, and if you're hoping for a first or last "Wow!" before or after the 350-plus other miles of coastal Oregon's scenic splendor, these few miles along the California border may be somewhat anticlimactic. That said, Brookings does have beautiful Azalea Park (which is gorgeous during the April–June spring bloom), and the popular, welcoming beachfront B&B rooms at **Lowden's,** just west of US-101 ($100 and up; 541/469-7045) offers direct access to a driftwood-strewn beach.

Just north of Brookings, one final piece of Oregon's abundant natural beauty has been preserved at **Harris Beach State Park,** across US-101 from the Oregon Welcome Center. Here you can walk down to a driftwood-laden beach and look out at numerous bird-infested islands.

Heading south, just over the California border from Brookings lies Redwood National Park, truly one of the West Coast's great places.

# CALIFORNIA

Stretching along the Pacific Ocean for roughly a thousand miles from top to tail, the California coast includes virgin wilderness, the cutting edge of cosmopolitan culture, and the full spectrum in between. For almost the entire way, coastal roads give quick and easy access to the best parts, with panoramic views appearing so often you'll simply give up trying to capture it all.

Starting in the north, the green forests of the Pacific Northwest continue well beyond the state border, forming a mountainous seaside landscape that lasts until the edge of metropolitan San Francisco. Along this stretch you'll find a number of old logging and fishing towns, varying from the burly blue-collar likes of **Eureka** and **Crescent City** to the upscale ambience of **Mendocino,** in and amongst endless acres of redwood forest.

At the approximate midpoint of the California coast sits **San Francisco,** deservedly ranked among the world's favorite cities. The 100 miles of coast stretching south from San Francisco hold numerous remnants of the Spanish and Mexican eras, exemplified by the town of **Monterey** and the beautiful mission at **Carmel.** Beyond here is another stretch of wild coastline, the rugged country of **Big Sur.**

Beyond the southern edge of Big Sur, opulent **Hearst Castle** marks the start of what most people consider Southern California, the rivers and trees of the north giving way to golden beaches, grassy bluffs, and considerably denser populations. A pair of very pleasant small cities, Midwestern-feeling **San Luis Obispo** and ritzy **Santa Barbara,** make excellent stops in themselves, smoothing the transition into the environs of **Los Angeles,** the unwieldy megalopolis that, seen from the I-5 freeway that links Los Angeles and **San Diego,** seems like one monstrous, 100-mile-long suburb. While it's true that the natural beauty that brought so many people to Southern California in the first place is increasingly endangered, some lovely, almost untouched places remain, hidden away but within easy access of the fast lane. We've pointed them out; enjoy them while they last.

## Jedediah Smith Redwoods State Park

The northernmost of the great redwood groves, **Jedediah Smith Redwoods State Park** covers nearly 10,000 acres of virgin forest along the banks of the Smith River. Stretching east of US-101, and most easily accessible from US-199, the park offers over 20 miles of usually uncrowded hiking trails through the pristine wilderness; it is considered by many the most perfect of all the redwood forests. One of the most enjoyable trails leads through **Stout Grove,** past the park's tallest tree and a number of summertime swimming holes along the Smith River.

The park is jointly managed by the state and federal governments, and you can get full hiking and camping information from the ranger station (707/458-3018) along US-199 at the main entrance to the park, four miles east of US-101. There's also a good **campground** (800/444-7275) with hot showers. For fans of roadside kitsch, there's one unique spot along US-101 in the hamlet of Smith River, 10 miles north of Crescent City: **Ship Ashore** (707/487-3141), a gift shop, restaurant, and motel along US-101, marked by a grounded ship.

## Crescent City

The county seat and largest city in Del Norte County, **Crescent City** (pop.

The Smith River and Jedediah Smith Redwoods State Park were named in memory of the legendary mountain man **Jedediah Strong Smith,** who in 1826 at the age of 27 led the first party of Americans overland to California. Smith also blazed the first trail over South Pass in Wyoming, later used by the Oregon Trail pioneers.

Outside Crescent City, California's most violent long-term criminals are kept behind bars in the state-of-the-art **Pelican Bay State Prison,** built in 1990.

4,006) is best treated as a base from which to explore the surrounding wilderness. The foggy weather that helps the redwoods thrive makes the city fairly depressing and gray, and what character it developed since its founding in 1853 has been eroded by storms; a giant tsunami, caused by the 1964 earthquake off Alaska, destroyed nearly the entire city.

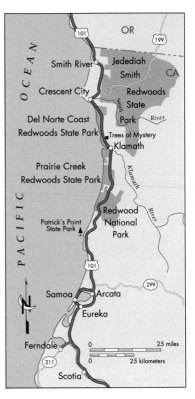

Crescent City includes the familiar lineup of motels and restaurants, plus local options like the **Beacon Burger** (707/464-6565), at 160 Anchor Way. Another only-in-California option is the **Curly Redwood Lodge,** 701 S. Redwood Highway ($55 and up; 707/464-2137), a nicely maintained 1950s motel made from a single, sawn-up redwood tree.

## Del Norte Coast Redwoods State Park

Spreading south from the Jedediah Smith redwoods, **Del Norte Coast Redwoods State Park** runs along the Pacific Ocean (and US-101) for about 10 miles, containing more than 6,000 acres of first- and second-growth redwoods as well as brilliant blooms of rhododendrons, azaleas, and spring wildflowers. Del Norte also protects miles of untouched coastline, the best stretch of which is accessible from the end of **Enderts Beach Road,** which cuts west from US-101 just north of the park entrance. From here, a 30-mile trail follows the coast to Prairie Creek.

The state park area is bounded on the south by an undeveloped section of **Redwood National Park.** Amongst the trees, the **HI Redwood Hostel** ($21 per person; 707/482-8265), 12 miles south of Crescent City and two miles north of the Trees of Mystery at 14480 US-101, is housed in a historic farm-house and offers cozy dormitory accommodations and a few private rooms.

## Trees of Mystery and Klamath

Hard to miss along US-101, thanks to the massive statues of **Paul Bunyan and Babe the Blue Ox** looming over the highway, the **Trees of Mystery** (daily 8 AM–dusk; $14; 707/482-2251) are literally and figuratively the biggest tourist draws on the Northern California coast.

Along the "Tall Tales Trail," chainsaw-cut figures, backed by audiotaped stories, stand in tableaux at the foot of towering redwoods. There's also a Sky Trail gondola lifting passengers up into the treetop canopy, a huge gift shop, and a small free museum of Native American art and artifacts.

Across the highway, **Motel Trees** (707/482-3152) has standard rooms from $60 and a coffee shop.

Along the banks of the mighty Klamath River, four miles south of the Trees of Mystery, the town of **Klamath** (pop. 650) is a brief burst of highway sprawl, support-ed by anglers who flock here for the annu-al fall salmon runs—provided there are any fish left to catch. Fisherfolk, walkers, and kayakers all avail themselves of the riverfront **Requa Inn** ($75 and up; 707/482-1425. At the south end of Klamath town, take a drive right through the **Tour-Thru Tree** ($2), then cross the Klamath River on a bridge graced by a pair of gilded cement grizzly bears.

All the land along the Klamath River is part of the extensive **Hoopa Valley Indian Reservation,** which stretches for over 30 miles upstream from the Pacific Ocean.

## Prairie Creek Redwoods State Park

The largest of the trio of north coast redwood parks, **Prairie Creek Redwoods State Park** is best known for its large herd of endangered **Roosevelt elk,** which you can usually see graz-ing in the meadows along US-101 at the center of the park, next to the main ranger station (707/465-7347). A modern freeway carries US-101 traffic around, rather than through, the Prairie Creek redwoods, so to reach the best sights, detour along the well-signed Newton B. Drury Scenic Parkway, which follows Prairie Creek along the old US-101 alignment through the heart of the park.

Another elk herd can be spotted among the coastal dunes at **Gold Bluffs Beach,** which stretches for 11 miles through untouched wilderness; there are trails leading from US-101, or you can follow Davison Road northwest from US-101, three miles south of the ranger station. Apart from the elk, Prairie Creek offers the usual mix of old-growth redwood trees, which here, more than in the other parks, mingle with dense growths of Sitka spruce and Douglas firs to form a near rainforest of greenery.

## Redwood National Park

Established in 1968, and later enlarged at a total cost of over $500 million, **Redwood National Park** protects some 100,000 acres of redwood forest, including the 30,000 acres previously preserved in the adjacent Smith, Del Norte, and Prairie Creek State Parks. To be honest, apart from the adjacent state parks, the trees preserved here aren't by any means the oldest, largest, or most beautiful; in fact, much of the federal parkland is second- or third-growth timber, clear-cut as recently as the 1960s. Though redwoods are the fastest-growing softwoods on earth—growing three to five feet a year when young—the groves here are rather disappointing compared to those in nearby areas and serve more as an environmental buffer zone than a tree-lover's pilgrimage site.

The groves of giant trees in Redwood National Park were used as a location for the Star Wars film **Return of the Jedi,** in which the characters cruised through the forest on airborne cycles. Patrick's Point played a starring role in the first **Jurassic Park.**

That said, Redwood National Park does hold two special sights, including the **Lady Bird Johnson Grove,** on Bald Hill Road a mile east of US-101, where the new park was dedicated in 1969. Ten miles farther up this road, and a long hike beyond that, the Tall Trees Grove holds the **world's tallest tree,** the 370-plus-foot Libbey Tree, whose trunk measures over 14 feet across.

At the south end of the park, the roadside-strip town of **Orick** stretches toward the coast, where the main Redwood National Park **visitors center** (707/465-7765) stands at the mouth of Redwood Creek.

## Patrick's Point State Park

If your idea of heaven is sitting on a rocky headland listening to the roar of the Pacific while watching the sunset or looking for passing gray whales, you won't want to pass by **Patrick's Point State Park** (707/677-3570). Three different 200-foot-high promontories at the heart of the park provide panoramic views, while the surrounding acres hold cedar and spruce forests (no redwoods), open pastures bright with wildflowers, great tidepools, a wide dark-sand beach, and two **campgrounds** (800/444-7275) with hot showers. There's also the preserved and restored remnants of a Yurok village, a redwood dugout canoe, and a garden of traditional herbs.

Continuing south, US-101 becomes a four-lane freeway along the ocean to Arcata and Eureka, but most of the old US-101 alignment winds along the cliff tops between Patrick's Point and the small town of Trinidad. Along this road you'll find some nice older motels, like the **Patrick's Point Inn** (707/677-3483 or 800/354-7006) at 3602 Patrick's Point Drive, just a half mile from the park entrance, with oceanside rooms from around $60 a night. Also here is the **Larrupin Cafe** (707/677-0230), at 1658 Patrick's Point Drive, which serves up bountiful portions of very fresh all-American food in a friendly, homey ambience—it's California cuisine without the snooty pretense you sometimes find farther south. It's open Thursday–Monday for dinner only and accepts only cash.

## Arcata

The most attractive and enjoyable town on the far north coast of California, **Arcata** (pop. 16,651) makes the best first (or last, depending upon the direction you're traveling) overnight stop south of the Oregon border. The presence of Humboldt State University's campus on the hills above US-101 accounts for the town's youthful, non-conformist energy, especially in the cafés, bookstores, bars, and crafts shops that surround the lively **Town Plaza,** two blocks west of US-101 at 9th and G Streets, incongruously graced by palm trees and a statue of President McKinley. The *Utne Reader* recently rated Arcata as "the most enlightened small town in California," and spending even a little time in this vibrant, cooperative Ecotopia may make you wonder whether or not you really do have to race back to the big-city 9-to-5 grind.

The author **Bret Harte** was run out of Arcata by angry townspeople in 1860, after writing an editorial in the local paper criticizing a massacre of a local Wiyot tribe.

Inland from Arcata along scenic US-299, the town of **Willow Creek** claims to be the heart of "Bigfoot Country," boasting a large statue of the furry beast to prove it. US-299 continues east over the coast range through the beautiful Trinity Alps to **Weaverville,** well-preserved site of a mid-1850s gold rush, before linking up with I-5 at Redding.

You can admire the town's many elaborate Victorian-era cottages, hunt wild mushrooms, clamber over sand dunes, or hike in the redwoods; afterward, relax with a cup of tea or, better yet, a soak in a hot tub at homey **Cafe Mokka,** the coast's only combo sauna and espresso bar, at 5th and J Streets (707/822-2228). Just off the plaza, **Jambalaya** serves burgers, mac 'n' cheese, ribs, and (of course) jambalaya at 915 H Street (707/822-4766), while microbrews flow from the taps of Arcata's amiable bars, many of which feature live music; for food, drink, and entertainment all under one roof, try the **Humboldt Brewery,** 856 10th Street (707/826-2739). For a complete selection of foodstuffs and supplies, and more insight into the local community, head to the large and stylish **North Coast Co-op,** at 8th and I Streets uphill from the plaza.

For a place to stay, the centrally located **Hotel Arcata** ($75 and up; 707/826-

0217 or 800/344-1221) is right on the plaza at 708 9th Street, or you can take your pick of the usual motels along US-101.

# Eureka

Evolving into a lively artists' colony from its roots as a fairly gritty and industrial port, **Eureka** (pop. 26,128) was well known to fur-trappers and traders long before it became a booming lumber and whaling port in the 1850s. Thanks to the lumber trade, Victorian Eureka grew prosperous, building elaborate homes, including the oft-photographed but closed to the public **Carson Mansion** along the waterfront at 2nd and M Streets, two blocks west of US-101. Along with dozens of well-preserved Victorian houses, Eureka has done a fine job of finding new uses for its many ornate commercial buildings, most of which have been preserved to house art galleries, cafés, and restaurants in what's now called **Old Town,** a half dozen blocks between the waterfront and US-101. This historic downtown quarter has a huge number of good places to eat and drink, including **Ramone's Bakery** (707/445-2923) at 209 E Street, the pub-like **Cafe Waterfront** (707/443-9190) at 1st and F Streets, and the popular **Sea Grill** (707/443-7187), a block from US-101 at 316 E Street. And if that's not enough to sate your appetite, for fish-and-chips and a pint or two of ale head along to the **Lost Coast Brewery,** 617 4th Street (707/445-4480).

One unique thing to see in Eureka is the collection of **Romano Gabriel Wooden Sculptures,** displayed in a plate-glass showcase at 315 Second Street. This brilliantly colorful folk-art extravaganza of faces and flowers originally stood in the front yard of local gardener Romano Gabriel, who made them out of discarded packing crates and other recycled materials over a period of some 30 years before his death in 1977.

Accommodation options range from roadside motels to upscale places like the **Carter House Inn** ($125 and up; 707/445-1390) at 1033 3rd Street, a re-created Victorian manor with spacious rooms and a big breakfast in the morning. For a more authentic Victorian experience, stay at one of California's most delightful B&Bs, the **Elegant Victorian Mansion** ($150 and up; 707/444-3144),

## Kinetic Sculpture Race

Arcata's creative community comes alive every Memorial Day weekend for the world-famous Kinetic Sculpture Race, in which participants pedal, paddle, and otherwise move themselves and their handmade vehicles on a multiple marathon across land and sea. Part art, part engineering, and part athletic competition, the Kinetic Sculpture Race is like nothing you've seen before. Beginning midday Saturday and running around the clock until Monday afternoon, a mind-boggling array of mobile contraptions—past winners have included everything from dragons and floating flying saucers to Egyptian pyramids (named Queen of Denial) and a Cadillac Coupe de Ville—make their way over land, sand, and sea from the town square of Arcata to the main street of Ferndale, twice crossing chilly Humboldt Bay.

Rule Number One of the Kinetic Sculpture Race is that all of the "sculptures" must be people-powered; beyond that, imagination is the primary guide. Many "rules" have developed over the years since the

"Just for the Halibut": racing along Samoa Peninsula

at 1406 C Street. A real treasure in a land of nice B&Bs, this magnificently restored 1888 Eastlake-style home has been opulently decorated with real antiques and Bradbury & Bradbury wallpapers by the hospitable Belgian-born innkeeper, Lily Vieyra.

For further information, contact the **Eureka! Humboldt County Convention and Visitors Bureau,** 1034 2nd Street (707/443-5097 or 800/346-3482).

## Samoa

Even if you're just passing through, don't miss the chance to visit the busy mill town of **Samoa,** across the bay from Eureka but easily reachable via the Hwy-255 bridge. Follow the signs past the piles of logs and belching mill chimneys to the unique race was first run in 1969, including such pearls as: "In the Event of Rain, the Race Is Run in the Rain," but most of these emphasize the idea that maintaining style and a sense of humor are at least as important as finishing the fastest. Since the Grand Prizes are valued at somewhere around $14.98, racers take part solely for the glory, but prizes are awarded in many categories: First- and last-place finishers are winners, and the racer who finishes in the exact middle of the pack gets the coveted Medio-Car Award—a broken-down old banger.

Spectators are expected to be active participants, too, so be prepared to shout and scream and applaud the competitors, or even jog or bike or kayak alongside them. There are many great vantage points along the route, but you have to be in the right place on the right day. The Kinetic Sculpture Race begins at noon on Saturday with a pre-race line-up around Arcata's Town Square, from where racers wind along country roads to the sandy Samoa Peninsula before spending the first night in downtown Eureka. Sunday morning the racers head across Humboldt Bay from Field's Landing, then camp out overnight along the ocean. Monday's trials include another water crossing and the muddy mess of the Slimy Slope, culminating in a mad dash down the Main Street of Ferndale surrounded by cheering multitudes. It's all good fun, and a great focus for a visit to this remarkable corner of the world.

**Samoa Cookhouse** (707/442-1659), built at the turn of the 20th century by the Louisiana Pacific lumber company, which still owns most of the peninsula. Inside the cookhouse, which is packed with logging memorabilia, take a seat at one of the 20-foot-long tables (redwood, of course, covered in checkered oil-cloth) and dig into the family-style feast. There are no menus, just huge platters of food at ridiculously low prices.

## Ferndale

Well worth the 10-mile detour west of US-101, the historic town of **Ferndale** (pop. 1,382) is an odd fish along the woodsy Northern California coast, a century-old dairy town that would look

The area around Ferndale has been hit by numerous **earthquakes,** including a destructive tremor in April 1992 that registered 6.9 on the Richter scale.

more at home in middle America. The three-block-long, franchise-free **Main Street** includes a fully stocked general store (the Golden Gait/Gate Mercantile), and white-washed farmhouses dot the pastoral valleys nearby. Ferndale's diverse history is well documented inside the **Ferndale Cultural Center** (hours vary; 707/786-4466), off Main Street at Shaw and 3rd Streets, where some of the wacky racers that take part in the annual Kinetic Sculpture Race (see sidebar) are displayed.

Ambling along Main Street is the best way to get a feel for Ferndale, and if you build up an appetite, there are many good places to eat. One of the oldest cafés in the West, **Poppa Joe's** (707/786-4180), is housed in a Victorian storefront at 409 Main Street, while the self-proclaimed "Oldest Hotel" is now a family-friendly Italian restaurant, **Ivanhoe** (707/786-9000), open for dinner only at 315 Main Street. Ferndale also boasts at least one high-end, destination-dining foodie favorite: **La Petite Maison,** a bistro and patisserie at 619 Main Street (707/786-4201).

Ferndale is equally well supplied with places to stay. Right off the heart of Main Street is the clean and tidy **Fern Motel,** 332 Ocean Avenue ($75; 707/786-5000), while for the full Victorian experience, *the* place to stay (or at least to see) in Ferndale is the lushly landscaped **Gingerbread Mansion,** at 400 Berding Street (707/786-4000), with deluxe rooms in a fabulously ornate home starting around $120 a night. Also nice is the **Shaw House** (707/786-9958), an 1854 American Gothic masterpiece with B&B rooms and bikes for rent at 703 Main Street.

## The Lost Coast

Between Ferndale and Mendocino, the main US-101 highway heads inland along the Eel River, but if you have time and a taste for adventure, head west from Ferndale along the narrow, winding Mattole Road, which loops around Cape Mendocino through the northern reaches of the so-called **Lost Coast,** a 100-mile stretch of shoreline justly famous for its isolated beauty. By road, you can only get close to the ocean at a few points—the few miles south of Cape Mendocino, and again at the fishing resort of **Shelter Cove,** west of Garberville—but hikers can have a field day (or week) exploring the extensive coastal wilderness. Some 50 miles of rugged, untouched coastline, packed with tidepools and driftwood-strewn beaches, have been preserved in a pair of parks, the **Kings Range National Conservation Area** in the north, and the **Sinkyone Wilderness State Park** farther south.

The Lost Coast area was the site of the first oil wells in California, which were drilled in the 1860s near the town of **Petrolia** but are now long gone.

Besides the Hwy-211/Mattole Road, which makes a 73-mile loop between Ferndale and the Rockefeller Forest section of Humboldt Redwoods State Park, a network of rougher and even more remote routes allows auto access to the Lost Coast, linking the hamlet of Honeydew with coastal Hwy-1 near Rockport. If you do explore this wild (and very rainy) region, take a good map and plenty of food and water, and be careful.

For further information on the Lost Coast, contact the **Bureau of Land Management** (707/825-2300); its office is at 1695 Heindon Road in Arcata.

## Scotia

Back along US-101, on the banks of the Eel River midway between the coast and the Humboldt Redwoods, **Scotia** is the only true company town left in California. The Pacific Lumber Company (a.k.a. "PALCO") built it and still owns every-

thing, from the two huge mills to the 10 blocks of pastel-painted houses, church, and schools that constitute this little community of about 1,000 people.

Stop first at the small **museum,** housed in the redwood Greek Revival former bank at the center of town, to pick up passes for self-guided **tours** (Mon.–Fri. 7:30 AM–2 PM; free) of the world's largest redwood mill. Following a yellow painted line through the mill at your own pace, you can gawk at (and listen to—it's a noisy business) every stage of the milling process. First, cut logs get de-barked by a powerful jet of water, then laser-guided band saws slice the logs into rough boards, which are turned into finished lumber. A raised catwalk runs through the center of the mill, and signs explain what's happening at each stage.

In summer, the rustic and historic **Winema Theater** screens new movies on weekends nights (plus an old-fashioned Saturday matinee). The one place to stay in town is the rustic **Scotia Inn** ($120 and up; 707/764-5683), which has B&B rooms and a very good restaurant; it's hard to miss at 100 Main Street, a block from the museum.

## Humboldt Redwoods State Park

Sheltering the biggest and best collection of giant coastal redwoods anywhere in the world, **Humboldt Redwoods State Park** is an exceptionally breathtaking corner of an exceptionally beautiful region. Covering 50,000 acres along the Eel River, this is the true heart of redwood country, containing the largest and most pristine expanses of virgin forest as well as some of the largest, tallest, and most remarkable trees.

Even if you're just passing through, be sure to turn onto the amazing **Avenue of the Giants,** 32 miles of old highway frontage between Jordan Creek and Phillipsville. This sinuous old road snakes alongside, and sometimes under, the faster and busier US-101 freeway, which is carried on concrete stilts through the park. At the north end of the park you'll find an impressive

The protection of the mighty redwood forests of Northern California was made possible not by the state or federal governments but primarily by the efforts of the **Save the Redwoods League,** a private organization that has raised, since its founding in 1918, millions of dollars to buy or preserve over 175,000 acres of redwood forest. To support these efforts, write to 114 Sansome Street, Room 605, San Francisco, CA 94104, or call 415/362-2352.

## Avenue of the Giants

The stretch of historic US-101 through the redwood country of Humboldt County, frequently called the "Avenue of the Giants," is lined by pristine groves of massive trees and provides boundless opportunities to come face-to-face with your own insignificance in nature's greater scheme of things. If you tire of this display of natural majesty, or simply want to keep it in context with the modern "civilized" world, you're in luck: Every few miles, amongst the stately trees, you'll come upon shameless souvenir stands selling redwood burl furniture and chainsaw sculptures, as well as wonderfully tacky tourist traps like the Legend of Bigfoot or Hobbittown USA, in Phillipsville. None of these is big or bold enough to detract from the main event— the big trees—and since they've been in operation since the early days of car-borne tourism, they're as much a part of the redwood experience as the trees themselves. Most charge only a few dollars' admission, so there's not a lot to lose.

While you're encouraged to stop at any and all of them—at least long enough to buy a postcard or two— the most tried-and-true attraction is the **Trees of Mystery,** marked by huge statues of Paul Bunyan and Babe the Blue Ox along US-101 in Klamath. Continuing south, the **One-Log House** in Phillipsville, is a mobile home carved from a single, 32-foot redwood log. In Myers Flat is the **Drive-Thru Tree,** 13078 Avenue of the Giants (old US-101), which wagon-borne travelers drove through more than a century ago. In the south, near the town of Leggett, are two more. One of the best stops in redwood country, **Confusion Hill** is one of those places where water runs uphill and the rules of physics seem not to apply; there's also a little railway train here that chugs uphill to a very nice grove of trees. Finally, at the **Chandelier Drive-Thru Tree,** south of Leggett off old US-101 on Drive-Thru Tree Road, drive your car through a 315-foot redwood tree, still growing strong despite the gaping hole in its belly.

at the end of Leggett, the "original" Drive-Thru Tree

collection of trees in the well-marked **Founders Grove,** where a half-mile nature trail leads past the 362-foot-tall, 1,600-year-old **Dyerville Giant,** lauded as the world's tallest tree before it fell during the winter of 1991. West of Founder's Grove, across US-101, the 13,000-acre **Rockefeller Forest** is one of the largest old-growth forests in the world and includes two of the park's champion trees, each over 360 feet tall and some 17 feet in diameter. In and amongst the natural wonders along the Avenue of the Giants are a handful of man-made ones: The **Eternal Treehouse** in Redcrest and the **Shrine Drive-Thru Tree** in Myers Flat are just two of the many good-natured "tourist traps" in this neck of the woods.

The best source of information on the park is the **visitors center** (707/946-2263), midway along the Avenue of the Giants in Weott; there's a pleasant state-run **campground** (800/444-7275) with showers right next door. You may have to drive a ways north (to Ferndale, Eureka, or Arcata) or south (to Garberville) from the park to find an exceptional meal, though there are a few nice places to stay, like the historic **Myers Country Inn** ($125 and up; 707/943-3259), midway along the Avenue of the Giants in Myers Flat. Farther south, the hamlet of Miranda holds the pleasant **Miranda Gardens Resort** ($50 and up; 707/943-3011), with motel rooms and rustic cabins.

## Garberville and Redway

Apart from its recurring presence in the national media during the occasional high-profile raids on local marijuana plantations, the redwood country town of **Garberville** is a pretty quiet, peaceful place. The US-101 freeway bypasses the town, and locals walk and talk to each other along the half dozen blocks of Redwood Drive, the well-signed business loop off the highway.

Enjoy an early-morning breakfast with the old-time locals at the **Eel River Cafe** at 801 Redwood Avenue (707/923-

3783), or an espresso and healthy food at the **Woodrose Café,** a block south at 911 Redwood Avenue (707/923-3191). Garberville also has all the motels you could want, including the **Motel Garberville** at 948 Redwood Drive ($60; 707/923-2422).

Just west of Garberville on the old highway, **Redway** is worth the short side trip for a late breakfast, lunch, or dinner at the **Mateel Cafe** (707/923-2030), a health-conscious gourmet haunt along Redwood Avenue at the center of town.

**Reggae on the River** festival, organized by the energetic Mateel Community Center (707/923-3368), attracts world-class performers and thousands of fans every summer.

Along US-101, four miles south of Garberville, one of the region's most characterful places is the stately **Benbow Inn** ($100–200; 707/923-2124), a circa-1926 mock Tudor hotel with a nice restaurant offering afternoon tea and scones on a sunny terrace overlooking Lake Benbow. The surrounding park often hosts live music and "living history" festivals.

## Leggett: The Drive-Thru Tree

No longer even a proverbial wide spot in the road since the US-101 freeway was diverted around it, **Leggett** marks the southern end of the Humboldt redwoods. At the south end of "town," a mile from the US-101/Hwy-1 junction along the old highway, stands one of the redwood region's most venerable and worthwhile roadside attractions, the "original" **Drive-Thru Tree** (daily 8 AM–dusk; $3). In addition to the famous tree, which had the hole cut through it in the 1930s, there's an above-average gift shop with a broad range of books, postcards, and schlocky souvenirs.

Nearby, the 16-acre grounds of the **River's Run Lodge** ($85 and up; 707/984-6321) has nine very quaint riverfront cabins, perfect for lazy days floating, swimming, or fishing. South of Leggett, US-101 runs inland racing toward San Francisco, while scenic Hwy-1 cuts west over the coastal mountains to Mendocino, winding slowly south along the Pacific.

The Garberville/Redway area is home to a pretty unusual community of old hippies and off-the-grid libertarians, who share their music and politics on non-commercial local radio station **KMUD 91.1 FM.**

## Rockport and Westport

From US-101 at Leggett, Hwy-1 twists up and over the rugged coastal mountains before hugging the coast through the weatherbeaten logging and fishing communities of **Rockport** and **Westport.** The small and informal **Howard Creek Ranch** ($125; 707/964-6725) in Westport offers comfortable B&B rooms, an outdoor hot tub, and easy access to the drift-wood-laden beach. (But be warned: it's a long way to a restaurant.) Farther south, **MacKerricher State Park** protects seven miles of rocky coast and waterfront pine forest; there's also a nice campground (800/444-7275).

## Fort Bragg

Cruising south along Hwy-1, 40 miles from Leggett and US-101, the first real town you come to is **Fort Bragg** (pop. 7,026), whose burly, blue-collar edge comes as something of a shock on the otherwise undeveloped, touristy Mendocino coast. Home to a large Georgia Pacific lumber mill and the region's largest commercial fishing fleet, Fort Bragg takes a  mostly no-frills approach to the tourist trade, leaving the dainty B&B scene to its upscale neighbor, Mendocino. However, there are a few down-to-earth places to eat: Very good omelettes and other eggy dishes are available at the appropriately named **Egghead's Restaurant** (707/964-5005) at 326 N. Main Street, while **The Wharf** (707/964-4283), along the Noyo River at 780 N. Harbor Drive, serves good-value seafood dinners. Perhaps the most popular place in town is **North Coast Brewing** (707/964-2739) at 455 N. Main Street, which serves good food and fine pints of its tasty Red Seal Ale.

From Fort Bragg, the **California & Western Railroad** runs a number of historic steam- and diesel-powered "Skunk Trains" over the mountains to Willits and back. Half-day and full-day trips ($35–50; 707/964-6372) run year-round.

Fort Bragg also boasts an unexpected treat: the best pizza for miles, at **Davelios,** 438 S. Franklin Street (707/964-4227).

Fort Bragg also has many inexpensive (by Mendocino standards, at least) motels, including the **Beachcomber Motel** ($59–199; 707/964-2402), at 1111 N. Main Street, which boasts the coast's only beachfront accommodation options (apart from camping). Another popular option is the **Old Coast Hotel,** 101 N. Franklin Street ($120 and up; 707/961-4488), an ornate Victorian-era inn (with a lively sports bar).

At the south edge of Fort Bragg, near the Hwy-20 junction and eight miles north of the town of Mendocino, 50 acres of intensely landscaped coastal hillsides tumble down between Hwy-1 and the ocean to form the **Mendocino Coast Botanical Gardens** (daily; $10; 707/964-4352), a nonprofit public space showing off the abundance of plant life that thrives in this mild, lush environment. Cultivated varieties like camellias, azaleas, roses, irises, fuchsias, and dahlias share space with native ferns, pines, redwoods, wildflowers, and wetland plants. It's also the only public garden in the USA that fronts right onto the ocean, so you can enjoy crashing waves and maybe even watch a gray whale spout offshore.

## Mendocino

One of the prettiest towns on the California coast (as seen in TV shows like *Murder, She Wrote* and numerous movies), **Mendocino** (pop. 1,100) is an artists' and writers' community par excellence. Now firmly established as an upscale escape for wage-slaving visitors from San Francisco (hence the local nickname, "Spendocino"), the town was originally established as a logging port in the 1850s. In recent years, Mendocino has successfully preserved its rugged sandstone coastline—great for wintertime whale-watching—while converting many of its New England–style clapboard houses into super-quaint B&B inns. The area is ideal for leisurely wandering, following the many paths winding through **Mendocino Headlands State Park,** which wraps around the town and offers uninterrupted views across open fields, heathers, and other coastal flora to the crashing ocean beyond. For field guides, maps, or a look at Mendocino in its lumbering heyday, stop by the **visitors center** (707/937-5804) in the historic Ford House at 735 Main Street.

Two miles north of town, one of the north coast's most perfect places is protected as **Russian Gulch State Park** (707/937-5804), where a waterfall, a soaring highway bridge, lush inland canyons, a swimming beach, and a impressive blowhole are

Mendocino

yours to enjoy along more than a mile of undisturbed coastline. There's camping, too, and sea kayaking, plus a fairly flat, three-mile paved bike trail, and miles of hiking.

Along with its many fine art galleries and bookshops, the town of Mendocino also has a delicious collection of bakeries, cafés, and restaurants. If you're not getting a breakfast at a B&B, come to the very friendly **Mendocino Cafe** at 10451 Lansing Street (707/937-6141), where locals have been starting their days for more than 20 years. Lunch or dinner at the **Moosse Cafe** (707/937-4323), at 390 Kasten at Albion Street, is always unforgettable. For a total splurge, try one of California's most famous (and expensive!) restaurants, **Cafe Beaujolais** (707/937-5614), two blocks from the waterfront at 961 Ukiah Street, which serves a prix fixe gourmet feast of California cuisine delicacies for dinner, nightly 6–9 PM.

Places to stay in Mendocino are rather expensive but generally delightful. The lovely **MacCallum House** ($150 and up; 707/937-0289), at 45020 Albion Street, includes a beautiful garden, good breakfasts, and a cozy nighttime bar and restaurant. Another place to stay is the circa-1858 **Mendocino Hotel** ($95 and up; 707/937-0511), on the downtown waterfront at 45080 Main Street.

## Van Damme State Park

Three miles south of Mendocino at the mouth of the Little River, **Van Damme State Park** stretches for five miles along the coastal bluffs and beaches and includes some 1,800 acres of pine and redwood forest. The park's unique attribute is the oddly contorted **Pygmy Forest,** a natural bonsai-like grove of miniature pines, cypress, and manzanita, with a wheelchair-accessible nature trail explaining the unique ecology. There's also a small, very popular campground, concession-guided ocean kayak tours, and a **visitors center** (707/937-0851) housed in a New Deal–era recreation hall.

The nearby hamlet of Little River is home to some rural-feeling, peaceful alternatives to Mendocino's in-town accommodations: the very comfy **Inn at Schoolhouse Creek** ($175 and up; 800/731-5525), where quaint cottages sit in eight acres of dog- and child-friendly gardens around a historic, oceanview home, and the luxurious, gourmet food-and-wine indulgence of the **Little River Inn** ($140 and up; 707/937-5942), where the same family has been welcoming travelers since 1939.

## Anderson Valley

From Hwy-1 south of Mendocino, Hwy-128 cuts diagonally across to US-101 through the lovely **Anderson Valley,** home to numerous fine wineries (including Husch, Navarro, and Kendall-Jackson) and the *Anderson Valley Advertiser,* one of California's most outspoken local newspapers. Anderson Valley also has its own regional dialect, called "Boontling," combining English, Scots-Irish, Spanish, and Native American words into a lighthearted lingo created, some say, simply to befuddle outsiders—or "shark the bright-lighters," in the local lingo.

To find out more, stop in the valley's tiny main town, **Boonville,** at the All That Good Stuff gift shop and ad-hoc information center, alongside the Horn of Zeese coffee shop. Fans of local food and wine will want to cross the highway to the **Boonville Hotel,** 14050 Hwy-128 ($125 and up; 707/895-2210), a wonderful restaurant (dinner only, alas) and wine bar. The historic building has upstairs rooms filled with art and furniture made by local craftspeople. Beer fans can make a pilgrimage east of town (toward Ukiah) to the solar-powered home of the **Anderson Valley Brewing Company,** 17700 Hwy-253 (707/895-BEER), where you can sample some of the world's best beers, including the legendary Boont Amber Ale.

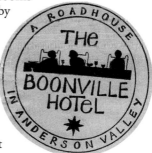

## Elk

While the coastal scenery is stupendous all the way along the Mendocino coast, one place worth keeping an eye out for on the drive along Hwy-1 is the tiny roadside community of **Elk** (pop. 450), 15 miles south of Mendocino. Elk is a wonderful little wide-spot-in-the-road, with what must be one of the oldest and most characterful service stations in California (the Elk Garage, in business since 1901) alongside a great little veggie-friendly breakfast-and-lunch road-food stop: **Queenie's Roadhouse Café** (707/877-3285). Elk also boasts a general store, some quirky cliffside cabins, and a steep trail leading down to the Pacific shore at Greenwood Cove.

## Point Arena and Gualala

The southernmost 40 miles of Mendocino coastline are almost totally undeveloped and virtually uninhabited, with green forests and coastal coves as far as the eye can see. The westernmost point here, **Point Arena,** is about five miles northwest of Hwy-1 via Lighthouse Road (the namesake lighthouse, built in 1870, stands 10 stories tall).

Another 15 miles south, situated at the very southern edge of Mendocino County, the old logging port of **Gualala** (pop. 1,500) has one truly remarkable feature: the Russian Orthodox domes of **St. Orres,** 36601 South Hwy-1 (707/884-3303), now a B&B inn and Francophile gourmet restaurant glowing with polished wood and stained glass, above Hwy-1 on the north side of town. Tiny Gualala has another culinary landmark as well: At the south end of town, just north of the Gualala River, **Pangaea** (Wed.–Sun. dinner only; 707/884-9669) is another of the coast's most popular restaurants, serving everything from beefy burgers to crab cakes with Thai curry sauce.

In between these two foodie haunts is a locally popular bar (with frequent live music) inside the **Gualala Hotel.** Great **camping** and an incredible coastal panorama can be yours at **Gualala Point Regional Park** (707/785-2377), on the south side of the Gualala River.

## Sea Ranch

Midway between Mendocino and the San Francisco Bay Area, the vacation-home community of **Sea Ranch** was laid out in the mid-1960s by an enthusiastic group of architects and planners including Lawrence Halprin and the late Charles Moore, who hoped to show that development need not destroy or negatively impact the natural beauty of the California coast. Strict design guidelines, preserving over half the 5,000 acres as open space and requiring the use of muted natural wood cladding and other barn-like features, made it an aesthetic success, which you can appreciate for yourself at the **Sea Ranch Lodge** ($160 and up; 707/785-2371), near the south end of the development.

The rest of Sea Ranch, however, is strictly private, which has raised the hackles of area activists, who after years of lawsuits finally forced through a few coastal access trails in the mid-1980s; these, such as **Walk-On Beach** at milepost 56.5, are marked by turnouts along Hwy-1.

## Salt Point State Park

The many sheltered rocky coves of **Salt Point State Park** make it ideal for undersea divers, who come to hunt the abundant abalone. Along these five miles of jagged shoreline, pines and redwoods clutch the water's edge, covering some 6,000 acres on both sides of Hwy-1 to make Salt Point a prime place for hiking and camping. For a guide to the 20 miles of trails, or background on the sandstone mortars and other remnants of the Pomo tribal village that stood here until the 1850s, contact the **visitors center** (707/847-3221).

One of the few positive effects of cutting down the native redwood forests that once covered the Northern California coast has been the emergence of giant-sized rhododendrons in their place. You'll find the most impressive display at the **Kruse Rhododendron Preserve,** high above Hwy-1 at the center of Salt Point State Park, where some 350 acres of rhododendrons, some reaching 15 feet in height, burst forth in late spring, usually peaking around the first week of May.

## Fort Ross State Historic Park

If you're captivated by California's lively history, one of the most evocative spots in the state is **Fort Ross State Historic Park,** the well-restored remains of a Russian fur-trapping outpost built here in 1812. During a 30-year residency, the Russians farmed wheat and potatoes, traded with native tribes, and trapped local seals and sea otters for their furs, which commanded huge sums on the European market. By 1840, the near-destruction of the sea otter population caused the company to shut down operations and sell the fort to Sacramento's John Sutter, who went bankrupt to finance the purchase. Later, the abandoned fort was badly damaged by the 1906 San Francisco earthquake and later fires, but the state has completed a high-quality restoration and re-

Russian Orthodox Chapel at Fort Ross

construction project, using hand-hewn lumber and historically accurate building methods to replicate the original barracks and other buildings, including a luminous redwood chapel.

Fort Ross spreads west from Hwy-1, 20 miles south of Sea Ranch and a dozen miles north of the Russian River. Outside the fort's walls, a modern **visitors center** (daily; $6 per car; 707/847-3286) traces the site's natural, native, and Russian history, and offers information on the park's many fine hiking trails.

## Jenner, Guerneville, and the Russian River

South of Fort Ross, Hwy-1 climbs high above the rugged coastline, offering breathtaking vistas of the Pacific Ocean hundreds of feet below. Twelve miles south of Fort Ross, Hwy-1 reaches the low-key resort community of **Jenner** (pop. 300), which stretches along the broad mouth of the Russian River. Harbor seals and sea lions sun themselves on the beach at Goat Rock, houses climb the steep hillsides, and there's also a gas station, a post office (inside a mobile home), and the excellent **River's End** (closed Tues. and Wed.; 707/865-2484), which has a range of great food (everything from burgers to Indonesian-spiced seafood) and oceanview tables (inside and outside, depending on the weather).

From Jenner, Hwy-116 runs east along the river, passing through forests, vineyards, and popular summertime resort

**Bohemian Grove,** the world's most exclusive men's club, covers 2,500 acres of redwood forest just south of the Russian River outside the village of Monte Rio.

In between Salt Point and Fort Ross, Beniamo Bufano's 72-foot *Peace* statue looms like a shiny silver missile alongside Hwy-1 above craggy **Timber Cove,** where there's also a nice restaurant and lodge (707/847-3231).

towns, the largest of which is **Guerneville,** 12 miles away, with a number of worthwhile cafés and a largely gay and lesbian summer population. A more traditional place, with a broad sandy beach, boat rentals, cabins, and riverfront camping, is **Johnson's** (707/869-2022) at 16241 1st Street. After 35-odd miles, Hwy-116 eventually links up with the US-101 freeway to and from San Francisco, providing a faster alternative to coastal Hwy-1.

## Sonoma Coast State Park

South of Jenner and the Russian River, Hwy-1 hugs the coast along 10 miles of rocky coves and sandy beaches, collectively protected as **Sonoma Coast Beaches State Park** (707/875-3483). Starting with Goat Rock at the southern lip of the Russian River mouth, a bluff-top trail leads south past intriguingly named and usually unpopulated pocket strands like Blind Beach, Schoolhouse Beach, Shell Beach, Wright's Beach (site of the park's main beachfront campground), and Salmon Creek Beach.

> While hiking along the Sonoma Coast, be careful: Many people have been drowned by **"sleeper" waves,** which rise unannounced and sweep people off the rocky shore.

At the southernmost end, Sonoma Coast Beaches State Park broadens to include the wildflower-covered granite promontory of **Bodega Head,** which juts into the Pacific and provides a great vantage point for watching the gray whale migrations in winter.

## Bodega Bay and Valley Ford

Protected by the massive bulk of Bodega Head, the fishing harbor of **Bodega Bay** has grown into an upscale vacation destination, with Sea Ranch–style vacation homes lining the fairways of golf resorts, and deluxe hotels overlooking the still-busy commercial wharves. On the waterfront, the **Lucas Wharf Deli** (707/875-3522) at 595 Hwy-1 dishes up fish-and-chips and clam chowder; the nearby **Tides Wharf** (707/875-3652) is bigger and has a large fresh-fish market.

South of Bodega Bay, Hwy-1 cuts inland around the marshy

coastal estuaries, passing by the photogenic small town of **Bodega,** whose church Alfred Hitchcock used for many of the scariest scenes in his 1960 movie, *The Birds.* The next town you pass through, **Valley Ford,** is another quaint little spot that holds a great old family-run roadhouse, **Dinucci's** (707/876-3260), serving huge portions of unreconstructed Italian food—minestrone, fresh bread, salad, and pasta—for around $12 per person—for dinner only, plus lunch on Sundays.

## Point Reyes

Between Bodega Bay and the Golden Gate Bridge, Hwy-1 slices through one of the country's most scenically and economically wealthy areas, **Marin County.** Though less than an hour from San Francisco, the northwestern reaches of the county are surprisingly rural, consisting of rolling dairylands and a few untouched small towns; Hwy-1 follows a slow and curving route along the usually uncrowded two-lane blacktop.

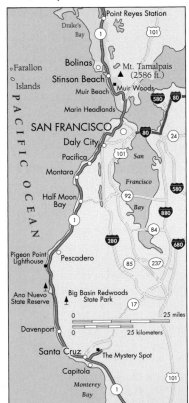

After looping inland south of Bodega Bay, Hwy-1 reaches the shore again at oyster-rich **Tomales Bay,** around which it winds for 20 miles before reaching the earthy but erudite town of **Point Reyes Station.** Here the excellent **Station House Cafe** (415/663-1515) at 3rd and Main Streets serves incredibly good breakfasts and delicious lunches that include great-tasting local oysters, on the half-shell or barbecued.

West from town along Sir Francis Drake Boulevard, the 74,000-acre **Point Reyes National Seashore** offers an entire guidebook's worth of hiking and cycling trails, broad beaches, dense forests, and more; stop at the Bear Valley **visitors center** (daily; free; 415/464-5100) for more information. The photogenic lighthouse at the tip of Point Reyes gives great views over the coast, and in winter and spring (Dec.–June) the steep headland

A sign outside the small white garage on **Main Street** in Point Reyes Station claims it is the oldest Chevrolet dealer in California.

makes an ideal spot for watching migrating gray whales.

Eight miles from the visitors center, the **HI-Point Reyes Hostel** (415/663-8811), at 1380 Limantour Road, has dorm beds in an old farmhouse on the road to Drake's Bay.

Dozens of delightful inns and restaurants operate in and around Point Reyes, but because they're a mere 20 miles from San Francisco, they're often booked solid weeks in advance. Everything from treetop rooms to waterfront cabins can be found through **Inns of Marin** (415/663-2000).

## Bolinas and Stinson Beach

Sitting at the southern end of the Point Reyes peninsula, **Bolinas** is a small town with a well-earned reputation for discouraging tourists; the signs leading you here from Hwy-1 are regularly torn down by locals bent on keeping the place—little more than a general store, a bakery, and a bar—for themselves. Bolinas also boasts one of the coast's best tidepool areas in **Duxbury Reef,** which curves around the western edge of Bolinas.

In contrast, the broad strands of **Stinson Beach,** four miles south along Hwy-1, are the Bay Area's most popular summertime suntanning spots. A grocery store and deli, the **Livewater Surf Shop** (which rents boards and the essential wetsuits), and a couple of outdoor bar-and-grills along Hwy-1 form a short parade at the entrance to the beach. The best place to eat hereabouts is the **Parkside Cafe** (415/868-1272), at 43 Arenal Avenue; if you want to stay overnight, try the basic but cheap **Stinson Beach Motel** ($65 and up; 415/868-1712), at 3416 Hwy-1.

If you have the chance to plan ahead, try to book a night at the **Steep Ravine**

**Cabins** (800/444-7275), just over a mile south of Stinson Beach on the ocean side of Hwy-1. Now part of Mt. Tamalpais State Park, these 10 rustic redwood cabins are very basic roofs-over-the-head (bring sleeping bags and food; water faucets are just outside the door) in an absolutely beautiful coastal chasm. These very popular cabins (originally owned by Bay Area big-wigs like Dorothea Lange) sleep up to five people and cost around $60 a night.

## Mt. Tamalpais, Muir Woods, and Muir Beach

The **all-terrain mountain bike,** which now accounts for half of all bikes on (and off) the roads, was invented in the late 1970s by a group of daredevil Marin cyclists intent on cruising down the fire roads of Mt. Tamalpais at the highest possible speed.

From the coast, a pair of roads—Panoramic Highway and the Shoreline Highway (Hwy-1)—twist up and over the slopes of **Mt. Tamalpais** (elev. 2,586), the signature peak of the San Francisco Bay Area. Known usually as "Mt. Tam," the whole mountain has been protected in semi-natural state within a series of state and national parks, and its voluptuous slopes offer incredible views of the urbanized Bay Area and the untouched coastline; drive to within 100 yards of the top for a 360-degree panorama, or stop at the Pan Toll **ranger station** (415/388-2070) for a map of Mt. Tam's hiking routes and fire roads.

A deep, dark valley between the coast and Mt. Tamalpais holds the last surviving stand of Marin County redwoods, preserved for future generations as the **Muir Woods National Monument** (daily 8 AM–dusk; $5), and named in honor of turn-of-the-20th-century naturalist John Muir. A paved, mile-long trail takes in the biggest trees, but since the park is often crowded with busloads of sightseeing hordes making the tour from San Francisco, you may want to explore the farther-flung areas, climbing up Mt. Tamalpais or following Muir Creek two miles downstream to the crescent-shaped cove of **Muir Beach,** along Hwy-1. Besides stunning scenery, Muir Beach is also home to the welcoming **Pelican Inn,** an "Olde English"–style pub serving food and fine beers; overnight guests get cozy rooms and access to a delightful "snug" fireplace (rooms $199 and up; 415/383-6000).

view from atop Mt. Tamalpais

Another enjoyably ersatz experience awaits at the junction of Hwy-1 and the US-101 freeway, where a historic roadside restaurant has been resurrected as the **Buckeye Roadhouse,** near Mill Valley at 15 Shoreline Highway (415/331-2600), where you can feast on fine barbecue, great steaks and burgers, and delicious desserts in a lively, retro–Route 66 atmosphere.

## Marin Headlands

If you can avoid the magnetic pull of the Golden Gate Bridge and San Francisco, take the very last turnoff from US-101 (northbound drivers take the second turnoff after crossing the bridge) and head west to the **Marin Headlands,** a former military base that's been turned back into coastal semi-wilderness. A tortuous road twists along the face of 300-foot cliffs, giving incredible views of the bridge and the city behind it. The road continues west and north to the **visitors center** (415/331-1540), housed in an old chapel, with a reconstructed Miwok shelter and details on hiking

> Every June since 1905, one of the country's wildest foot races, the **Dipsea,** has followed a rugged 7.1-mile route from the town of Mill Valley over Mt. Tamalpais to Stinson Beach. For more information, call the Dipsea hotline at 415/331-3550.

and biking routes. And if you're so inclined, on Wednesday–Friday afternoons you can tour the world's only restored Cold War–era Nike missile silo (free).

Nearby, the barracks of old Fort Barry have been converted into the very peaceful **HI-Marin Headlands Hostel** (415/331-2777), which has dorm beds and private rooms for around $22 per person.

## Across San Francisco

From the north, Hwy-1 enters **San Francisco** across the glorious **Golden Gate Bridge,** where parking areas at both ends

# San Francisco

San Francisco is easily the most enjoyable city in the United States. Its undulating topography turns every other corner into a scenic vista, while its many distinctive neighborhoods are perfect for aimless wandering. Museums document everything from Gold Rush history to cutting-edge modern art, while stellar restaurants offer the chance to sample gourmet food from around the world—all in an easily manageable, densely compact small city.

If there's one place in the city you should stop to get your bearings, it's **Fort Point,** a massive, photogenic Civil War fort standing along the bay, directly beneath the Golden Gate Bridge. You can wander at will through the honeycomb of corridors, staircases, and gun ports, watch the fearless surfers and windsurfers offshore, and take in a panoramic view of the City by the Bay. From here you can walk up to and across the Golden Gate Bridge, or head west to Land's End or back into town via a popular bayfront walking and cycling trail. Another great place to get a feel for San Francisco is **Golden Gate Park,** which stretches inland from the western edge of the city, including more than 1,000 acres of gardens, a boating lake, and two landmark museums, featuring the copper-clad art of the De Young Museum, and the natural history, aquarium, and planetarium of the grass-roofed Academy of Sciences.

If there's one other place that ought to be on your S.F. itinerary, it's **Alcatraz.** Aptly known as The Rock, this was America's most notorious prison from 1934 until 1963. Now preserved as a historical park, the island is worth a visit as much for the views of San Francisco as for its grim past. To reach Alcatraz, take one of the ferries that leave throughout the day from Pier 41 at the east end of Fisherman's Wharf.

The **San Francisco Giants** (tickets $40 and up; 877/4SF-GTIX) play at retro-modern AT&T Park, along the bay in downtown's South of Market district.

# Practicalities

San Francisco is one of the few cities on the West Coast where you really don't need a car, since distances are short and public transportation is quite extensive; the grid street plan makes it easy to find your way around. San Francisco's Municipal Railway's ("Muni"; 415/673-6864) network of public transit buses, trams, and cable cars will take you all over the city.

The only problem for visitors in San Francisco is deciding where to eat—there are so many great places that choosing among them can be a painful process. For breakfast, **Sears Fine Foods** (415/986-1160) at 439 Powell Street on Union Square is a local institution, as is the upscale **Fog City Diner** (415/982-2000) at 1300 Battery Street, which serves gourmet comfort food (and the world's best french toast) in a stainless steel supper club. Two more S.F. culinary landmarks are the **Swan Oyster Depot** (weekdays till 6 PM only; 415/673-1101 or 415/673-2757), a half block north of the California Street cable car at 1517 Polk Street, a simple oyster bar serving the city's freshest shellfish and coldest Anchor Steam beer; and **Sam's Grill** (415/421-0594), downtown at 374 Bush Street, with incredible grilled meat and fish dishes, melt-in-your-mouth shoestring fries, and ancient-looking 1930s wooden booths that seem like set pieces from a Sam Spade mystery.

Given San Francisco's worldwide popularity, it's no surprise that room rates run pretty high—expect to pay around $200 a night (including taxes). If you're here for a honeymoon or other romantic reason, the nicest place in town is the swanky **Mandarin Oriental** ($350 and up; 415/276-9600) at 222 Sansome Street, which fills the top floors of a Financial District skyscraper and has 270-degree bay views (even from the bathtubs!). The best budget options are the two HI hostels, one on the bay at Fort Mason (415/771-7277), another downtown at 312 Mason Street (415/788-5604); both cost about $25 a night. In between there are some nice motels on the outskirts of downtown, like the nouveau retro **Hotel del Sol** ($129 and up; 415/921-5520), in the Marina District at 3100 Webster Street.

The **San Francisco Convention and Visitors Bureau** (415/974-6900) publishes a good free street map and offers extensive listings of attractions, accommodations, and restaurants.

the opening of the Golden Gate Bridge, 1937

let you ditch the car and walk across the elegant two-mile-long span. South from the bridge, Hwy-1 follows 19th Avenue across Golden Gate Park, then runs due south through the outer reaches of San Francisco, finally reaching the coast again at the often-foggy town of Pacifica. The most scenic alternate is the **49-Mile Drive,** the best part of which heads west from the bridge through **Presidio National Park,** along Lincoln Boulevard and Camino del Mar, following the rugged coastline to **Land's End,** where you can hike around and explore the remains of Sutro Baths, eat at the wonderful new Cliff House, or experience the wonders of the Camera Obscura.

From Land's End, this scenic route runs south along the oceanfront Great Highway, which eventually links back up with Hwy-1 near the small but enjoyable **San Francisco Zoo** (daily; $11; 415/753-7080).

Since driving and parking in San Francisco can be frustrating and expensive (Steve McQueen could never make *Bullitt* in today's traffic!), consider parking out here in the 'burbs and taking public transportation into the center of town. The N Judah MUNI trolley line runs between downtown and the coast just south of Golden Gate Park, where parking is comparatively plentiful.

## Montara and Princeton

From the San Francisco city limits, Hwy-1 runs along the Pacific Ocean through the rural and almost totally undeveloped coastline of San Mateo County. The first eight miles or so are high-speed freeway, but after passing through the suburban communities of Daly City and Pacifica, the pace abruptly slows to a scenic cruise. **Pacifica,** which has a long pier, a popular surfing beach, a bowling alley, an oceanview Taco Bell, and a handy Holiday Inn Express motel, makes a good edge-of-town base for seeing the San Francisco area; south of here, two-lane Hwy-1 hugs the decomposing cliff tops for the next few miles before reaching **Montara,** where the old but still functioning lighthouse has been partly converted into the **HI-Point Montara Hostel** (650/728-7177).

South of Montara, Hwy-1 bends inland around the rugged shores of the **James Fitzgerald Marine Preserve** (650/728-3584), a wonderful (but very fragile) tidepool area filled with anemones and other delicate sea creatures. The tidepools are visible at low tide only; look, but don't touch! Hwy-1 continues south past the marina at Princeton-by-the-Sea, where you can enjoy a different sort of sealife appreciation: the fresh fish-and-chips (plus nice wines and cold beers) at **Barbara's Fish Trap** (cash only; 650/728-7049).

# Half Moon Bay

The first sizable coastal town south of San Francisco, **Half Moon Bay** is 25 miles from the city but seems much more distant. A quiet farming community that's slowly but surely changing into a Silicon Valley suburb, Half Moon Bay (pop. 12,000) still has an all-American Main Street a block east of the Hwy-1 bypass, lined by hardware stores, cafés, bakeries, and the inevitable art galleries and B&Bs. The main event here is the annual **Pumpkin Festival,** held mid-October, which celebrates the coming of Halloween with a competition to determine the world's largest pumpkin—winning gourds weigh as much as a half ton!

Until the construction of the monstrous carbuncle of the beachfront Ritz-Carlton, the coastline of Half Moon Bay was almost completely undeveloped, but it's still pretty nice and accessible, with a four-mile-long string of state park beaches (camping and hiking info, 650/726-8819) at the foot of blufftop farms and ranches. The

Looking for the world's biggest waves? Head down to **Maverick's,** an offshore reef area a half mile off Pillar Point, three miles north of Half Moon Bay. In winter, when conditions are right, 35-foot mega-waves draw expert surfers from all over the world. For a report, and a safety advisory to warn off any wannabes, call **Maverick's Surf Shop** at 650/726-0469; it's located at 530 Main Street in Half Moon Bay.

town also retains its rural feel, but with significantly better restaurants. The best fish tacos (and great fish-and-chips) can be had at the **Flying Fish Grill** (650/712-1125), at the north end of Main Street, while excellent and not outrageously expensive Italian specialties are on the menu at **Pasta Moon,** 315 Main Street (650/726-5125).

## Pescadero and Pigeon Point Lighthouse

The 50 miles of coastline between Half Moon Bay and Santa Cruz are one of the great surprises of the California coast: The virtually unspoiled miles offer rocky tidepools and driftwood-strewn beaches beneath sculpted bluffs topped by rolling

Pigeon Point Lighthouse

green fields of brussels sprouts, artichokes, and "U-Pick" berry patches. Access to the water is not always very easy, and while surfers seem to park along Hwy-1 and walk across the fields to wherever the waves are breaking, for visitors it's best to aim for one of the half dozen state parks, like San Gregorio, Pomponio, Bean Hollow, or Año Nuevo.

The biggest town hereabouts, **Pescadero** (pop. 500) is a mile or so inland from Hwy-1 and well worth the short detour for a chance to sample the fresh fish, great pies, and other home-cooked treats at **Duarte's Tavern,** 202 Stage Road (650/879-0464), open daily for breakfast, lunch, and dinner at the south end of the block-long downtown.

Ten miles south of Pescadero, the photogenic beacon of **Pigeon Point Lighthouse** has appeared in innumerable TV and print commercials; the graceful, 115-foot-tall brick tower is open for tours (Sun. 10 AM–3 PM; donation), and the adjacent lighthouse quarters function as the very popular **HI-Pigeon Point Hostel** (650/879-0633), which has dorms beds, family-friendly private rooms, and a hot tub perched above the crashing surf.

## Año Nuevo State Reserve

West of Hwy-1, one of nature's more bizarre spectacles takes place annually at **Año Nuevo State Reserve** (8 AM–dusk daily; $7 per car; 650/879-2025), where each winter hundreds of humongous northern elephant seals come ashore to give birth and mate. The males reach up to 20 feet head-to-tail, weigh as much as three tons, and have dangling proboscises that inspired their name. These blubbery creatures were hunted almost to extinction for their oil-rich flesh. In 1920, fewer than 100 were left in the world; their resurgence to a current population of more than 100,000 has proved that protection does work.

Every December, after spending the summer at sea, hordes of male elephant seals arrive here at Año Nuevo, the seals' primary onshore rookery, ready to do battle with each other for the right to procreate. It's an incredible show, with the bulls bellowing, barking, and biting at each other to establish dominance; the "alpha male" mates with most of the females, and the rest must wait till next year. Pups conceived the previous year are born in January, and mating goes on through March. During the mating season, ranger-led **tours** ($7; 800/444-4445) are the only way to see the seals; these tours are very popular, so plan ahead and try to come midweek. The three-mile walk from the parking area to the shore is worth doing at any time of year, since it's a very pretty scene and some of the seals are resident year-round.

The only accommodation option along this stretch of coast is three miles south of the lighthouse, or two miles north of the entrance to Año Nuevo, at **Costanoa** ($150 and up; 650/879-1100). A stylish retro-modern eco-minded resort, open since 1999 on the inland side of Hwy-1, Costanoa has everything from a luxurious lodge to tent cabins (complete with saunas!). There's also a café and an adjacent KOA campground (650/879-7302).

Though the San Mateo coastline is quite beautiful, the waters are very cold—and home to a hungry population of **great white sharks,** which have been known to attack surfers as well as seals.

Midway between Año Nuevo State Reserve and Santa Cruz, the **Davenport Cash Store,** on the east side of Hwy-1 in the village of Davenport, serves hearty breakfasts and lunches. Tiny Davenport is also the birthplace of the Odwalla fresh fruit-juice company.

## Big Basin Redwoods State Park

The oldest and largest of California's state parks, **Big Basin Redwoods State Park** ($7 per car; 831/338-8860) protects some 16,000 acres of giant coastal redwoods. Established in 1902, the park has many miles of hiking and cycling trails high up in the mountains. The heart of the park is most easily accessible from Santa Cruz via Hwy-236, but a popular trail winds up from the coast to the crest, starting from Hwy-1 at **Waddell Creek Beach,** a popular haunt for kite-surfers and sailboarders, who sometimes do flips and loops in the wind-whipped waves.

## Santa Cruz

The popular beach resort and college town of **Santa Cruz** (pop. 54,593) sits at the north end of Monterey Bay, a 90-minute drive from San Francisco, at the foot of a 3,000-foot-high ridge of mountains. Best known for its Boardwalk amusement park, which holds the oldest surviving wooden roller coaster on the West Coast, and for the large University of California campus in the redwoods above, Santa Cruz takes its name from the ill-fated mission settlement begun here in 1777 but wiped out by an earthquake and tidal wave in 1840. Modern Santa Cruz was all but leveled by another earthquake in 1989 but has since recovered its stature as one of the more diverting stops on the California coast.

**Natural Bridges State Park,** two miles north of Santa Cruz via West Cliff Drive, has a natural wave-carved archway and, in winter, swarms of monarch butterflies.

The downtown area lies a mile inland, so from Hwy-1 follow the many signs pointing visitors toward the wharf and the beach, where plentiful parking is available. Walk, rent a bike, or drive along the coastal Cliff Drive to the world's first **Surfing Museum** (Wed.–Mon. noon–4 PM; donations), which is packed with giant old redwood boards and newer high-tech cutters, as well as odds and ends tracing the development of West Coast surfing. Housed in an old lighthouse, it overlooks one of the state's prime surfing spots, Steamer Lane, named for the steamships that once brought day-tripping San Franciscans to the wharf.

A large part of the Santa Cruz economy still depends upon visitors, and there are plenty of cafés, restaurants, and accommodation options to choose from. Eating and drinking places congregate west of Hwy-1 along Front Street and Pacific Avenue in downtown Santa Cruz, which has a number of engaging, somewhat countercultural book and record shops along with cafés like **Zoccoli's** (831/423-1711) at 1534 Pacific Avenue, which has great soups and sandwiches. The best burgers, veggie burgers, and fries are a block west of Pacific at **Jack's Hamburgers,** 202 Lincoln Street (831/423-4421). More good veggie food can be had at the **Saturn Café,** 145 Laurel Street (831/429-8505), while the stylish **Soif** wine bar at 105 Walnut Avenue (831/423-2020) has fine wines and tasty tapas-like treats.

> Santa Cruz has just about fully recovered from the 1989 **Loma Prieta earthquake,** which had its epicenter in the hills southeast of the city.

Motels line Hwy-1, and some nice-looking Victorian-era B&Bs stand atop Beach Hill, between the Boardwalk and downtown, where the **Seaway Inn,** 176 West Cliff Drive ($125 and up; 831/471-9004) is nice, clean, and reasonably priced. You can also avail yourself of the

Surfboard designs have come a long way.

**HI-Santa Cruz Hostel** (831/423-8304) at 321 Main Street, with dorm beds in an immaculate 1870s cottage for less than $20 per person. Among the many nice B&Bs is the rustic **Babbling Brook** ($189 and up; 831/427-2437 or 800/866-1131) at 1025 Laurel Street.

## Santa Cruz Boardwalk

The bayfront **Santa Cruz Boardwalk** should really be your main stop; besides the dozens of thrill rides and midway games, it boasts the art deco Cocoanut Grove ballroom, where throughout the summer swing bands still play the sounds of the 1930s and 1940s, and two rides that are such classics of the genre they've been listed as National Historic Landmarks. The biggest thrill is the **Giant Dipper** roller coaster, open since 1924, a senior citizen compared to modern rides but still one of the Top 10 coasters in the country—the clattering, half-mile-long tracks make it seem far faster than the 40 mph maximum it reaches. Near the roller coaster is the beautiful

the roller coaster at Santa Cruz

Charles Looff **carousel,** one of only six left in the country, with 70 hand-carved wooden horses doing the same circuit they've followed since 1911; grab for the brass rings while listening to music pumped out by the 342-pipe organ, imported from Germany and over 100 years old.

Along with these and many other vintage arcade attractions, the amusement park also features a log flume ride, a sky ride, a two-story miniature-golf course installed inside the old bathhouse, plus a bowling alley and all the shooting galleries, laser tag, and virtual reality machines you could want. The Boardwalk, which has a concrete concourse but retains a great deal of charm and character, is open daily in summer, and weekends only during the rest of the year. Admission is free and individual rides vary in cost, with the Giant Dipper costing about $4 a trip and all-day, all-ride passes priced about $30. For more information, call 831/423-5590.

## Mystery Spot

In the hills above Santa Cruz, two miles east of Hwy-1 at 1953 Branciforte Drive, the **Mystery Spot** (daily; $5; 831/423-8897) is one of those fortunate

few tourist traps that actually gets people to come back again. Like similar places along the Pacific coast, the Mystery Spot is a section of redwood forest where the usual laws of physics seem not to apply (trees grow in oddly contorted corkscrew shapes, and balls roll uphill). Among those who study vortexes and other odd geomantic places, the Mystery Spot is considered to be the real thing, but you don't have to take it seriously to enjoy yourself.

## Watsonville, Castroville, and Moss Landing

Between Santa Cruz and Monterey, Hwy-1 loops inland through the farmlands fronting Monterey Bay. Part freeway, part winding two-lane road, Hwy-1 races through, and to be honest there's not a lot worth stopping for: The beaches can be dreary, and the two main towns, Watsonville and Castroville, are little more than service centers for the local fruit and vegetable packers, though Castroville—where in 1947 then-unknown **Marilyn Monroe** reigned as "Miss Artichoke" during Castroville's Artichoke Festival, still celebrated each September—does have one odd sight: the "World's Largest Artichoke," a concrete statue outside a very large fruit stand at the center of town.

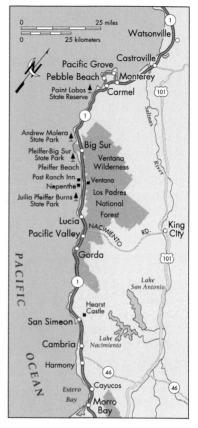

Back on the coast, midway along Monterey Bay, the port community of **Moss Landing** is a busy commercial fishery, with lots of trawlers and packing plants—not to mention pelicans aplenty. Moss Landing sits alongside Elkhorn Slough, the largest wetlands area in Monterey Bay, and is home to the research arm of the Monterey Bay Aquarium, to an obtrusively huge electricity generating plant, and to **The Whole Enchilada** (831/633-3038), which has spicy seafood and a popular Sunday jazz brunch right on Hwy-1, just south of the power plant.

Much of the bayfront north of Monterey formerly belonged to the U.S. Marine Corps base at Fort Ord. Almost the entire parcel was turned over to the State of California to house the **California State University at Monterey Bay,** which opened its doors in 1995.

Coastal farms along **Monterey Bay** grow nearly 85 percent of the nation's artichokes, which you can sample along with other produce at stands along Hwy-1.

## San Juan Bautista

Away from the coast, 15 miles inland from Monterey Bay via Hwy-129 or Hwy-156, stands one of California's most idyllic small towns, **San Juan Bautista** (pop. 1,549). It centers upon a grassy town square bordered by a well-preserved mission complex, complete with a large church and monastery, standing since 1812. Two other sides of the square are lined by hotels, stables, and houses dating from the 1840s through 1860s, preserved in their entirety within a state historic park (daily; $2; 831/623-4881).

Completing the living history lesson, the east edge of the square is formed by one of the state's few preserved stretches of El Camino Real, the 200-year-old Spanish colonial trail that linked all the California missions with Mexico. Adding to the interest, the trail runs right along the rift zone of the San Andreas Fault, and a small seismograph registers tectonic activity. (Incidentally, San Juan Bautista was where the climactic final scenes of Hitchcock's *Vertigo* were filmed—though in the movie, they added a much more prominent bell tower with a seemingly endless staircase.)

The town's Main Street is a block from the mission and is lined by a handful of antique shops, Mexican restaurants, and cafés like the **Mission Cafe** at 300 3rd Street (831/623-2635).

North of San Juan Bautista, at the southern fringe of the Bay Area's famed Silicon Valley, **Gilroy Gardens** at 3050 Hecker Pass Road (daily in summer only; $30; 408/840-7100), is five different gardens on 100-plus acres, offering a taste of everything from early California agriculture to topiary animals—plus a few thrill rides, of course.

## Monterey

The historic capital of California under the Spanish and Mexican regimes, **Monterey** (pop. 31,954), along with its peninsular neighbors Carmel and Pacific Grove, is one of the most satisfying stops in California. Dozens of significant historical sites have been well preserved, most of them concentrated within a mile-long walk called the Path of History that loops through the compact downtown area. Park in the lots at the foot of Alvarado Street, Monterey's main drag, and start your tour at **Fisherman's Wharf,** where bellowing sea lions wallow in the water, begging for popcorn from tourists. Next stop should be the adjacent **Custom House,** the oldest governmental building in the state, recently restored as the **Monterey State Historic Park visitors center** (daily;

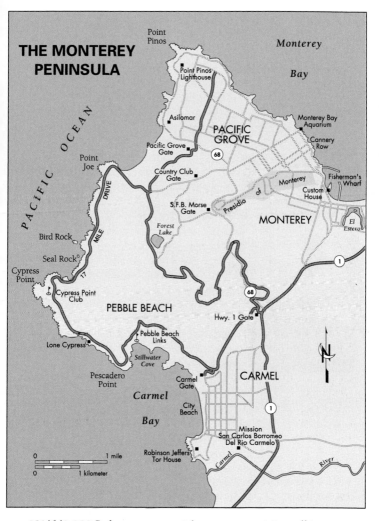

THE MONTEREY
PENINSULA

Monterey
Bay

Point
Pinos

Point Pinos
Lighthouse

Asilomar

Monterey Bay
Aquarium

Cannery
Row

PACIFIC
GROVE

Pacific Grove
Gate

68

Fisherman's
Wharf

Point
Joe

Country Club
Gate

Monterey

Custom
House

S.F.B. Morse
Gate

Presidio of

MONTEREY

El
Estero

Forest
Lake

Bird Rock

Seal Rock

Cypress
Point

Cypress Point
Club

PEBBLE BEACH

Hwy. 1 Gate

68

1

Lone Cypress

Pebble Beach
Links

Stillwater
Cove

Carmel
Gate

CARMEL

Pescadero
Point

Carmel

City
Beach

1

Bay

N

Mission
San Carlos Borromeo
Del Rio Carmelo

0        1 mile

0    1 kilometer

Robinson Jeffers
Tor House

Carmel          River

831/649-2836); here you can pick up maps or join walking tours
of old-town Monterey.

From the Custom House, which is now surrounded by the
modern Doubletree Hotel complex, you can follow the old railroad right-of-way west along the water to **Cannery Row,** where
abandoned fish canneries have been gussied up into upscale bars
and restaurants—most of them capitalizing on ersatz
Steinbeckian themes. The one real attraction here is the excellent
**Monterey Bay Aquarium,** 886 Cannery Row (daily; $29.95;

The internationally famous **Monterey Jazz Festival** is held every year at the end of summer. For performers, dates, and other information, phone 800/307-3378.

Along Hwy-1 on the northwest edge of Monterey, the elegant **Hotel Del Monte,** a grand resort that attracted the first wealthy tourists in the 1880s, is now part of the large **U.S. Navy Postgraduate School.**

NATIONAL
**STEINBECK**
CENTER

The writer John Steinbeck lived in and around the Monterey Peninsula for many years and set many of his stories here, though things have changed so much in recent years that his beloved Cannery Row is hard to recognize. Steinbeck was born and is buried in **Salinas,** east of Monterey on US-101; after spurning him for most of his lifetime, the town recently opened the **National Steinbeck Center** at 1 Main Street as a memorial to its literary son.

831/648-4800), housed in a spacious modern building and loaded with state-of-the-art tanks filled with over 500 species of local sealife. The aquarium is rated by many as the best in the world: Displays let visitors touch tidepool denizens, watch playful sea otters, gaze into the gently swaying stalks of a three-story-tall kelp forest, be hypnotized by brilliantly colored jellyfish, or face truly weird creatures that usually live thousands of feet below the surface of the bay.

## Monterey Practicalities

Because Monterey gets such a considerable tourist trade, there's no shortage of restaurants, though good food at reasonable prices can be hard to find. In the historic center of town, one good bet is the **Old Monterey Café,** 489 Alvarado Street (831/646-1021), serving large portions at breakfast and lunch. For breakfast near the aquarium, try **First Awakenings,** 125 Ocean View Blvd (831/372-1125). For seafood, catch an early-bird special (before 6 PM) at one of the dozen restaurants on the wharf— **Cafe Fina** (831/372-5200) has the best food, including good pizzas. Also good is the **Monterey Fish House,** west of downtown at 2114 Del Monte Avenue (831/373-4647). Top of the scale is flashy **Montrio** (831/648-8880), located at 414 Calle Principal, which serves San Francisco–style grilled chicken and fish in a converted fire station.

Places to stay vary widely, starting with the **HI-Monterey Hostel** ($21 per person; 831/649-0375), in historic Carpenters Union Hall off Cannery Row at 778 Hawthorne Street, four blocks from the aquarium. Moderate motels line Munras Street along the old US-101 highway frontage south toward Carmel, while prices in downtown Monterey hover in the $200 range. One exception to the generally high prices is the refurbished and centrally located **Monterey Hotel** ($100 and up; 831/375-3184 or 800/727-0960) at 406 Alvarado. Near the Wharf is the beachfront **Monterey Bay Lodge** ($125 and up; 831/372-8057).

Many other nice places to stay and eat can be found in neighboring Pacific Grove or Carmel. For additional information on destinations from Monterey south to Big Sur, contact the Monterey County **visitors bureau** (831/649-1770 or 877/MONTEREY).

## Pacific Grove

Perched at the tip of the Monterey Peninsula, **Pacific Grove** (pop. 16,117) is a quiet throwback to old-time tourism, dating from the late 1880s when the area was used for summertime Methodist revival meetings. The revivalists' tents and camps later grew into the West Coast headquarters of the populist Chautauqua educational movement, based in upstate New York. The town still has a curiously Midwestern feel, from its many small churches to the rows of well-maintained Victorian cottages lining its quiet streets. Besides the many fine old buildings, the best reason to come here is the beautiful, fully accessible shoreline, which boasts some of the coast's best tidepools, sunset views, and endless opportunities for winter whale-watching.

Pacific Grove is the best known of about 20 places in California where millions of monarch butterflies spend the winter months. From October until March, the butterflies congregate on the **"Butterfly Trees,"** a grove of pines on Ridge Road off Lighthouse Avenue, well signed from downtown.

Pacific Grove's main street, Lighthouse Avenue, runs through the 15-mph commercial district of galleries, movie theaters, and cafés like **Toastie's** (831/373-7543), a comfy breakfast and lunch place at 702 Lighthouse Avenue. Nearby **Pepper's** (831/373-6892), at 170 Forest Avenue, serves very good, fresh Mexican food, while a range of fairly priced fish dishes are on the menu at **The Fishwife** (831/375-7107), overlooking **Asilomar State Beach** at 1996 Sunset Drive.

Places to stay in Pacific Grove are more reasonably priced than in Monterey or Carmel: **Andril's Fireplace Cottages** ($150 and up; 831/375-0994), is a lovingly maintained set of old-fashioned motor-court cabins, all with fireplaces and just two blocks from the ocean at 569 Asilomar Boulevard. Rustic **Asilomar Conference Center** ($95 and up; 831/372-8016), at 800 Asilomar Boulevard, has a modern lodge and some lovely, woodsy, Julia Morgan–designed cabins, but the former YWCA summer camp is often filled with church groups or convention-goers. For a romantic getaway, it's hard to beat the jointly run pair of Victorian-era B&Bs overlooking the Pacific from Lover's Point: **Grand View** and **Seven Gables** ($175 and up; 831/372-4341), at 555–557 Ocean View Boulevard.

One event that brought Pebble Beach to national attention was the annual golf tournament hosted by Bing Crosby; originally an informal get-together, it grew into one of the main events of the professional circuit and is now the **AT&T Pebble Beach National Pro-Am** held each winter.

Every August for nearly 50 years, Pebble Beach has drawn classic car collectors from around the world to show off their immaculately restored automobiles at the annual **Concours d'Elegance.**

## 17-Mile Drive and Pebble Beach

Spanning the coast between Pacific Grove and Carmel, the **17-Mile Drive** is one of the most famous toll roads in the nation. Opened in the 1880s, the route initially took guests of Monterey's posh Hotel Del Monte on a scenic carriage ride along the coast through the newly planted Del Monte Forest between Carmel and Pacific Grove. Guided by Samuel F. B. Morse, son of the inventor, the formerly wild area underwent development beginning in the 1920s, first with golf courses like Pebble Beach and Cypress Point, and since then with resort hotels and posh homes.

Enter the drive at any of the gates, where you'll pay the toll ($9.50, bicyclists are free, and motorcyclists are banned) and be given a map and guide to the route, pointing out all the scenic highlights, especially the trussed-up old **Lone Cypress,** legally trademarked subject of so many Carmel postcards. It's definitely worth doing the drive, if only to say you have, but to be honest, the views from the drive are no more or less splendid than they are from the toll-free drives, like Ocean View Boulevard in Pacific Grove, Scenic Drive in Carmel, or Hwy-1 through Big Sur. You do, however, get to stop at the Lodge, where your toll will be deducted from the price of lunch or dinner. If you're in the mood to splurge on wanton luxthe Lone Cypress

ury, you can also stay overnight at either of two extremely plush golf and tennis resorts: the modern, suburban-style country club of the **Inn at Spanish Bay,** which is also home to an Ansel Adams photography gallery, or the stately, old-money **Lodge at Pebble Beach.** Both resorts charge upwards of $500 a night; for details on accommodations (or Pebble Beach golf fees and tee times), call 831/647-7500.

## Carmel

The exclusive enclave of **Carmel-by-the-Sea** (to give its complete name) began life in the early years of the 20th century as a small but lively bohemian colony inhabited by the literary likes of Sinclair Lewis, Mary Austin, and Upton Sinclair. However, with a few arts-and-craftsy exceptions, by the 1950s Carmel had turned into the archly conservative and contrivedly quaint community it is today—a

Carmel's leading light, **Clint Eastwood,** seems ever-present: Besides once serving as mayor, he owns the Carmel Mission Ranch resort. As a filmmaker, he used Carmel as the location for one of his most disturbing movies, the psychopathic 1970s *Play Misty for Me.*

place where Marie Antoinette would no doubt feel at home, dressing down as a peasant, albeit in Chaps by Ralph Lauren. Preserving its rural feel by banning street addresses (and skateboards and home mail delivery . . . ), Carmel simultaneously loves and abhors the many thousands of tourists who descend on it every weekend to window-shop its many designer boutiques and galleries that fill the few blocks off Ocean Avenue, the main drag through town. Though most of Carmel's many art galleries seem directed at interior decorators, a few are worth searching out, including the **Photography West Gallery** on the southeast corner of Dolores and Ocean Streets, and the **Weston Gallery** on Sixth Avenue near Dolores Street, featuring the works of Edward Weston, Ansel Adams, and other Carmel-based photographers.

Though it's easy to be put off by the surface glitz, Carmel does have a lot going for it. The water is too cold and treacherous for swimming, but broad **City Beach** at the foot of Ocean Avenue gleams white against a truly azure cove. To the south, aptly named **Scenic Drive** winds along the rocky coast, past poet Robinson Jeffers's dramatic **Tor House** (tours Fri. and Sat. 10 AM–3 PM; $7; 831/624-1840). Jeffers, who lived here between 1914 and 1962, built much of what you see here out of boulders he hauled up by hand from the beach.

At the south end of the Carmel peninsula, another broad beach spreads at the mouth of the Carmel River; this usually unpopulated spot, part of **Carmel River State Park,** is also a favorite spot for scuba divers exploring the deep undersea canyon.

Above the beach, just west of Hwy-1 a mile south of central Carmel, **Carmel Mission** (daily; donations) was the most important of all the California missions, serving as home, headquarters, and final resting place of Father Junípero Serra, the Franciscan priest who established Carmel and many of the 20 other California missions, and who is entombed under the chapel floor. The gardens—where on weekends wedding parties alight from limos to take family photos—are beautiful, as is the facade with its photogenic bell tower. This is the mission to visit if you visit only one.

## Carmel Practicalities

Dozens of good and usually expensive restaurants thrive in Carmel, but one place to see, even if you don't eat there, is the tiny, mock-Tudor **Tuck Box Tea Room** (closed Mon. and Tues.; 831/624-6365), on Dolores Street near 7th Avenue. Rebuilt after a fire but still dollhouse-cute, it serves up bacon-and-eggs breakfasts and dainty plates of shepherd's pie and Welsh rarebit for lunch. If you'd rather join locals than mingle with your fellow tourists, head to **Katy's Place** (daily 7 AM–2 PM; 831/624-0199) on Mission Street between 5th and 6th, serving delicious waffles and some of the world's best eggs Benedict. For great, MSG-free Szechuan Chinese food at low prices (and minimal ambience), check out **Tommy's Wok,** on Mission between Ocean and 7th Avenue (831/624-8518).

Carmel has only one place to stay approximating a budget option, the very pleasant **Carmel River Inn** (831/624-1575 or 800/882-8142), just west of Hwy-1 near the Carmel Mission, but away from here rates average well over $250 a night.

However, if you want to splurge on a bit of luxury, Carmel is a good place to do it. Besides the golf course resorts of nearby Pebble Beach, Carmel also has the commodious, 1920s-era, mission-style **Cypress Inn** at Lincoln and 7th ($200 and up; 831/624-3871 or 800/443-7443), partly owned by dog-loving Doris Day (and featuring posters of her movies in the small bar off the lobby). A relaxing spot away from downtown is the historic, Clint Eastwood–owned **Carmel Mission Ranch** ($150 and up; 831/624-6436 or 800/538-8221) at 26270 Dolores Street, within walking distance of the beach and mission and offering full resort facilities and a very good restaurant.

## Point Lobos State Reserve

The sculpted headland south of Carmel Bay, now protected as **Point Lobos State Reserve** (daily; $10 per car; 831/624-4909), holds one of the few remaining groves of native Monterey cypress, gnarled and bent by the often stormy coastal weather. The name comes from the barking sea lions (*lobos del mar*) found here by early Spanish explorers; hundreds of seabirds, sea lions, sea otters, and—in winter—gray whales are seen offshore or in the many picturesque, sea-carved coves.

The entrance to the reserve is along Hwy-1, three miles south of Carmel Mission, but in summer the park is so popular that visitors sometimes have to wait in line outside the gates. If possible, plan to come early or during the week. Whenever you can, come: Point Lobos has been lauded as the greatest meeting of land and sea in the world, and crowded or not it's definitely a place you'll want to see. Point Lobos has endless vistas up and down the rocky coast, and if you don't mind a short hike, there are a number of magical beaches hidden away at its southern end.

The northern stretches of Big Sur are marked by the rugged coves, redwood forests, and sandy beach at Garrapata State Park, four miles south of Point Lobos, and the massive volcanic hump of **Point Sur,** 19 miles south of Carmel, a symmetrical dome capped by a 100-year-old lighthouse.

# Big Sur

Stretching 90 miles south of Carmel from Point Lobos all the way to Hearst Castle, Big Sur is one of the most memorable sections of coastline on the planet, with 5,000-foot-tall mountains rising up from the Pacific Ocean. Early Spanish missionaries dubbed it El País Grande del Sur (the Big Country of the South), and the rugged land has resisted development or even much of a population—the current total of around 1,500 is roughly the same as it was in 1900, and for the 3,000 years before that.

Hwy-1, the breathtaking drive through Big Sur, was finally cut across the very steep cliffs in 1937 after 20 years of convict labor and several fatalities. Named the state's first scenic route—so dedicated by Lady Bird Johnson in 1966—it's an incredible trip. Like the Grand Canyon and other larger-than-life natural wonders, Big Sur boggles the mind and, in an odd way, can be hard to handle; you have to content yourself with staring in awestruck appreciation, taking pictures, or maybe toasting the natural handiwork with a cold beer or glass of wine at one of the few but unforgettable cafés and restaurants along the way.

However beautiful the drive along Hwy-1, it's also narrow, twisting, packed with sluggish RVers on holiday weekends, and often closed by mud slides and washouts during torrential winter storms, and the even more destructive wildfires that have plagued the coast in recent summers. In 1983, the biggest storm in recent memory closed the road for more than a year, and in 1998, 70 miles of it were blocked for over four months, and scars from the 2008 fires can be seen inland from Big Sur Village.

Big Sur is still a very wild place (with little or no cell phone reception), and there are very few services, with most of the overnight accommodations booked up solidly during the peak summer season. Spring brings wildflowers, while fall gets the most reliably good weather. No matter when you come, even if you just drive through in an afternoon, be sure to stop whenever possible and get out of the car; scenic viewpoints line the roadside, and dozens of trails lead off into the wilds. The best basic guide to Big Sur is an annual free newspaper, *El Sur Grande,* published by Monterey County and available at ranger stations and many other locations in and around Big Sur.

## Andrew Molera State Park

Spreading along the coast at the mouth of the Big Sur River, 21 miles south of Carmel, **Andrew Molera State Park** is a grassy former cattle ranch on the site of one of Big Sur's oldest homesteads. In the 1850s, immigrant John "Juan Bautista" Roger Cooper bought the land and built a cabin, which still stands along Hwy-1 near the park entrance. Well-blazed trails wind along both banks of the river down to the small beach, horses are available for hire (831/625-5486), and there are quite a few nice places to **camp** (walk-in only). In winter, the park is also a popular resting spot for migrating monarch butterflies.

## Big Sur Village

South of Andrew Molera, Hwy-1 cuts inland toward the heart of **Big Sur,** the deep and densely forested valley carved by the Big Sur River. Consisting of little more than three gas stations, a couple of roadside markets, and a number of lodges and restaurants, the mile-long village of Big Sur (pop. 950) represents the only real settlement between Carmel and Hearst Castle.

The photogenic **Bixby Creek Bridge,** 15 miles south of Carmel, was the largest concrete bridge in the world when it was built in 1932. The old coast road runs along the north bank of the creek, linking up again with Hwy-1 near Andrew Molera State Park.

At the north end of "town," the **Big Sur River Inn** (831/667-2700) has a woodsy, warm, and unpretentious restaurant overlooking the river, and rooms upstairs and across the highway. Next door is a small complex that includes crafts galleries, a grocery store with burrito bar, and the homey **Maiden Publick House** (831/667-2355), which features good beers, pizzas, and pub grub. Continuing south, the next mile of Hwy-1 holds Big Sur's nicest group of rustic cabins and campgrounds along the river: **Ripplewood** (831/667-2242) also has a café, a gas station and general store.

At the south end of the Big Sur village, a classic 1950s motor court has been restored, with period furnishings and free Wi-Fi, to its original glory as the **Glen Oaks Motel** ($125 and up; 831/667-2105).

## Pfeiffer–Big Sur State Park

Roughly a half mile south of Big Sur village, **Pfeiffer–Big Sur State Park** is the region's main event, an 810-acre riverside forest that's one of the most pleasant (and popular) parks in the state. Besides offering a full range of visitor services—restaurant, lodge, riverside campground, and grocery store—the park includes one of Big Sur's best short hikes, a two-mile loop on the Valley View trail that takes in stately redwoods as well as oak and madrone groves, a 40-foot waterfall, and a grand vista down the Big Sur valley to the coast.

The park also has the main **ranger station** (831/667-2315) for all the state parks in the Big Sur area. Just south of the park entrance, a USFS **ranger station** (831/667-2423) on the east side of Hwy-1 has information on hiking and camping opportunities in the mountains above Big Sur, including the isolated (but poison oak–ridden) **Ventana Wilderness.**

## Pfeiffer Beach

South of Pfeiffer–Big Sur State Park, halfway up a long, steep incline, a small road turns west and leads down through dark and heavily overgrown Sycamore Canyon, eventually winding up at Big Sur's best beach, **Pfeiffer Beach.** From the lot at the end of the road, a short trail runs through a grove of trees before opening  onto the broad white sands, loomed over by a pair of hulking offshore rocks. The water's way too cold for swimming, but the half-mile strand is one of the few places in Big Sur where you can enjoy extended beachcombing strolls. The beach's northern half attracts a clothing-optional crew, even on cool, gray days.

The landmark red farmhouse along Hwy-1 at the entrance to Ventana was built in 1877 by pioneer rancher **W. B. Post,** whose descendants developed the Post Ranch Inn.

## Ventana and the Post Ranch Inn

South of Sycamore Canyon, roughly three miles from the heart of Big Sur village, Hwy-1 passes between two of California's most deluxe small resorts. The larger of the two, **Ventana** (around $500; 831/667-2331 or 800/628-6500), covers 1,000 acres of Big Sur foothills and offers saunas, swimming pools, and four-star accommodations in 1970s-style cedar-paneled rooms and cabins. There's also a very fine restaurant, "Cielo," with incredible views and reasonable prices, to which guests are ferried in a fleet of electric carts.

Completed in 1992 and directly across Hwy-1 from Ventana, the **Post Ranch Inn** ($500 and up; 831/667-2200 or 800/527-2200), a low-impact but ultra-high-style luxury resort hanging high above the Big Sur coast, is at the forefront of luxury ecotourism. In order to preserve Big Sur's untarnished natural beauty, the Post Ranch Inn is designed to be virtually invisible from land or sea: The 24 accommodations—all featuring a king-size bedroom and a whirlpool bath with built-in massage table—blend in with the landscape, disguised either as playful tree houses raised up in the branches of the oaks and pines, or as underground cabins carved into the cliff top. The Post Ranch restaurant, Sierra Mar, is also excellent, or if you want to have a look and plan for a future escape, free tours of the resort are given Monday–Friday at 2 PM.

> In 1987, the mighty **California condor** was all but extinct in the wild. Now, thanks to a successful captive breeding and reintroduction program, these massive birds can be seen soaring over the Ventana Wilderness that rises above Big Sur.

## Nepenthe

One of the most popular and long-lived stopping points along the Big Sur coast, **Nepenthe** (831/667-2345) is a rustic bar and restaurant offering good food and great views from atop a rocky headland a thousand feet above the Pacific. Named for the mythical drug that causes one to forget all sorrows, Nepenthe looks like something out of a 1960s James Bond movie, built of huge boulders and walls of plate glass. The food is plenty good—burgers, steaks, and fried fish dominate the menu—but it's the view you come here for.

Sharing a parking lot, and taking advantage of similar views, the neighboring **Cafe Kevah** (831/667-2344) serves a veggie-friendly range of soups, salads, and quesadillas, plus good teas and coffees and microbrews on a rooftop deck; you'll find a gift shop downstairs selling top-quality arts and crafts and knitwear by Kaffe Fassett, who grew up here and whose family owns the place.

> The hilltop where Nepenthe now stands was previously the site of a rustic cabin that **Orson Welles** bought for his wife, **Rita Hayworth,** in 1944.

Right along Hwy-1, at a sharp bend in the road just south of Nepenthe, the **Henry Miller Memorial Library** (irregular hours, usually daily in summer; 831/667-2574) carries an erratic but engaging collection of books by and about the author, who lived in Big Sur for many years in the 1950s.

A half mile south of Nepenthe on the east side of the highway, one of the oldest and most atmospheric places to stay is **Deetjen's Big Sur Inn** ($80–180; 831/667-2377), a rambling and rustic redwood lodge built by a Norwegian immigrant in the 1930s and now a nonprofit, preservationist operation. Deetjen's also serves Big Sur's best breakfasts and hearty dinners.

## Julia Pfeiffer Burns State Park

**Julia Pfeiffer Burns** was a Big Sur pioneer whose family lived near Pfeiffer Beach and homesteaded much of this rugged, isolated area. In 1915, she married John Burns, a Scottish orphan who lived with the nearby Post family, and they continued to live and ranch at what is now Julia Pfeiffer Burns State Park until Julia's death in 1928.

If for some untenable reason you only have time to stop once along the Big Sur coast, **Julia Pfeiffer Burns State Park** (dawn–dusk daily) should be the place. Spreading along both sides of Hwy-1, about 14 miles south of Big Sur village, the park includes one truly beautiful sight: a slender waterfall that drops crisply down into a nearly circular turquoise-blue cove. This is the only waterfall in California that plunges directly into the Pacific.

From the parking area, east of the highway, a short trail leads under the road to a fine view of the waterfall, while another leads to the remnants of a pioneer mill, complete with a preserved Pelton wheel. Other routes climb through redwood groves up to the chaparral-covered slopes of the Santa Lucia Mountains.

About six miles south of Nepenthe, or a mile north of the parking area at Julia Pfeiffer Burns State Park, a steep fire road drops down to **Partington Cove,** where ships used to moor in the protected anchorage. The last stretch of the route passes through a 100-foot-long tunnel hewn out of solid rock.

# Lucia and the Nacimiento Road

The southern reaches of the Big Sur coast are drier and more rugged, offering bigger vistas but fewer stopping places than the northern half. The road winds along the cliffs, slowing down every 10 miles or so for each of three gas station/café/motel complexes, which pass for towns on the otherwise uninhabited coast. The first of these, 25 miles south of Big Sur village, is **Lucia,** which has a very good restaurant and lantern-lit cabins. High on a hill just south of Lucia, marked by a slender black cross, is the Benedictine **New Camaldoli Hermitage,** open to interested outsiders as a silent retreat. For details, phone 831/667-2456.

Five miles south of Lucia, the narrow Nacimiento Road makes an unforgettable climb up from Hwy-1 over the coastal mountains. Though ravaged in places by wildfires, it's a beautiful drive, winding through hillside chaparral and dense oak groves before ending up near King City in the Salinas Valley. One real highlight here is **Mission San Antonio de Padua** (daily 8 AM–5 PM; 831/385-4478), a well-preserved church and monastery that is still in use by a Catholic religious community. Because the road passes through sections of Fort Hunter-Liggett Army Base, you may need to show valid car registration and proof of insurance.

Near the foot of the Nacimiento Road are two of the most accessible oceanside campsites in Big Sur: **Plaskett Creek** and **Kirk Creek,** operated by the U.S. Forest Service (831/667-2423).

Continuing south, Hwy-1 runs through **Pacific Valley,** the hills above which are a popular hang-gliding spot, then passes by a number of small but pretty beaches and coves before reaching **Gorda,** the southernmost stop on the Big Sur coast. Just north of Gorda, tucked away east of the highway, **Treebones Resort** ($135 and up; 831/424-4787) offers rustic yurts and a swimming pool. South of Gorda, a series of small state parks lines the highway, but the next services are 25 miles farther south in San Simeon, at the entrance to Hearst Castle.

Three miles south of Julia Pfeiffer Burns State Park, the New Age **Esalen Institute** offers a variety of "Human Potential" workshops; it also has an incredible set of natural hot springs, right above the ocean and sometimes open to the public midnight–5 AM. For information or reservations, phone 831/667-3000.

The roadside along Hwy-1 in the southern half of Big Sur has been invaded by thick bunches of **pampas grass** that crowd out local flora.

# San Simeon: Hearst Castle

At the south end of Big Sur, the mountains flatten out and turn inland, and the coastline becomes rolling, open-range ranch land. High on a hill above Hwy-1 stands the coast's one totally unique attraction, **Hearst Castle.** Located 65 miles south of Big Sur village and 43 miles northwest of San Luis Obispo, Hearst Castle is the sort of place that you really have to see to believe, though simple numbers—144 rooms, including 36 bedrooms—do give a sense of its scale.

Even if Hearst's taste in interior design (or his megalomania, which by all accounts was understated in his fictional portrayal in Orson Welles's *Citizen Kane*) doesn't appeal, Hearst Castle cries out to be seen. One of this century's most powerful and influential Americans (the Rupert Murdoch of his day), Hearst inherited the land, and most of his fortune, from his father George Hearst, a mining mogul, and began work on his castle following the death of his mother in 1919. With the help of the great California architect Julia Morgan, who designed the complex to look like a Mediterranean hill town with Hearst's house as the cathedral at its center, Hearst spent 25 years work-ing on his "castle"—building, rebuild-ing, and filling room after room with furniture—all the while entertaining the great and powerful of the era, from Charlie Chaplin to Winston Churchill.

William Randolph Hearst

A small **museum** (daily; free) in the visitors center, next to where you board the trams that carry you up to the house, details Hearst's life and times. If you want to go on a **tour,** the Experience Tour (Tour 1, which costs $25) gives the best first-time overview, taking in the main house and the two swimming pools, plus a 45-minute movie giving the background on Hearst and his house-building. Other tours (2, 3, and 4) specialize in different aspects of the house and gardens; each tour costs $25 and takes around two hours. Advance reservations (800/444-4445) are all but essential, especially in summer.

Since Hearst Castle is rather isolated, it's a good idea to stay the night before or after a visit at nearby San Simeon, which has grown into a massive strip of motels. One of the nicest ones here is the **San Simeon Lodge** ($50–150; 805/927-4601) at 9520 Castillo Drive.

## Cambria

Without Hearst Castle, **Cambria** would be just another farming town, but being next to the state's number-two tourist attraction (after Disneyland) has turned Cambria into quite a busy little hive. Apart from a few hokey, tourist-trapping souvenir shops at the north end of town, it's a casual, walkable, and franchise-free community of arts and crafts galleries, boutiques, and good restaurants; from Hwy-1, Main Street makes a three-mile loop around to the east, running through the heart of town.

Above Cambria, a folk-art landmark known as **Nitt Witt Ridge** ($10; 805/927-2690) was built by the eccentric artist Art Beal, who used old Busch beer cans, seashells, roof tiles, and broken-down car parts to build, over 50 years starting in the late 1920s, what is often called a "Poor Man's Hearst Castle." The sprawling three-story house, with great views and intriguing details, is now open for tours at 881 Hillcrest Drive.

Back in town, hearty breakfasts are available at the **Redwood Cafe** (805/927-4830) at 2094 Main Street, while well-prepared multi-ethnic and vegetarian food is on the menu at **Robin's** (805/927-5007), a half block off Main Street at 4095 Burton Drive. For barbecue, check out the **Main Street Grill** (805/927-3194), at 603 Main Street. Places to stay range from nice older motels like the **Bluebird Inn** ($90 and up; 805/927-4634), at 1880 Main Street, to the spacious suites and cabins at rustic **Cambria Pines Lodge** ($140 and up; 805/927-4200), on a hill above Hwy-1 at 2905 Burton Drive.

Five miles south of Cambria, **Harmony** (pop. 18) is a former dairy town turned arts and crafts colony, with a range of galleries and a small wedding chapel. Another diverting little town, **Cayucos,** sits along the coast 10 miles farther south.

## Morro Bay

Marked by the Gibraltar-like monolith of Morro Rock, which was noted by Juan Cabrillo in 1542 and now serves as a peregrine falcon preserve and nesting site, **Morro Bay** (pop. 10,350) surrounds a busy commercial fishing harbor, a half mile west of Hwy-1. A thin, six-mile-long strip of sand protects the bay from the Pacific Ocean, forming a seabird-rich lagoon that's included within **Morro Bay State Park,** a mile southeast of Morro Rock. There's an excellent museum ($2) with displays on local wildlife, and the park also contains the friendly **Bayside Cafe** (805/772-1465), serving lunch and dinner. Next door, when the weather's nice, you

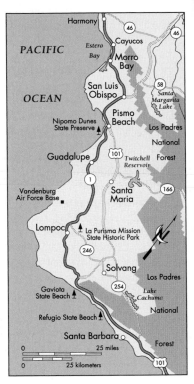

can rent **kayaks** ($6 an hour) and paddle around the estuary.

The rest of Morro Bay is pretty quiet; one unusual sight is a giant **outdoor chessboard** (with waist-high playing pieces), at the foot of Morro Bay Boulevard on the waterfront in City Park. For clam chowder or fish-and-chips, try **Giovanni's,** 1001 Front Street (805/772-2123), while good fast Mexican-themed "fusion" food is available at the **Taco Temple,** an often crowded and grandly named fish shack on the north side of Morro Rock at 2680 Main Street (805/772-4965).

The **James Dean memorial,** 27 miles east of Paso Robles near the junction of Highways 46 and 41, is the site where the talented and rebellious actor crashed in his silver Porsche and died on September 30, 1955.

## San Luis Obispo

Located midway between San Francisco and Los Angeles at the junction of Hwy-1 and US-101, **San Luis Obispo** (pop. 44,174) makes a good stopping-off point, at least for lunch if not for a lengthier stay. Like most of the towns along this route, San Luis, as it's almost always called, revolves around an 18th-century mission, here named **Mission San Luis Obispo de Tolosa.** Standing at the heart of town, at Chorro and Monterey Streets, the mission overlooks one of the state's liveliest small-town downtown districts, with dozens of shops and restaurants backing onto Mission Plaza, a two-block park on the banks of Mission Creek.

Besides the mission and the lively downtown commercial district that surrounds it, not to mention the nearly 25,000 students buzzing around the nearby campus of Cal Poly San Luis Obispo, San Luis holds a singular roadside attraction, the **Madonna Inn** ($150 and up; 805/543-3000 or 800/543-9666), which stands just west of US-101 at the foot of town. One of California's most noteworthy pop culture landmarks, the Madonna Inn is a remarkable example of what architecturally minded academic types like to call vernacular kitsch. Created by local contractor Alex Madonna, who died in 2004, the Madonna Inn offers over 100 unique rooms, each decorated in a wild barrage of fantasy motifs: There are the bright pink honeymoon suites known as "Just Heaven" and "Love Nest," the "Safari Room" covered in fake zebra skins with a jungle-green shag carpet, and the cave-like "Cave Man Room." *Roadside America* rates it as "the best place to spend a vacation night in America," but even if you can't stay, at least stop for a

Another San Luis landmark, **the world's first motel,** opened at 2223 Monterey Street in 1925. Originally called the Milestone Motel, the Spanish revival structure was later renamed the **Motel Inn,** but it went out of business long ago and now stands next to US-101 on the grounds of the Apple Farm restaurant and motel.

# El Camino Real and the California Missions

While the American colonies were busy rebelling against the English Crown, a handful of Spaniards and Mexicans were establishing outposts and blazing an overland route up the California coast, along the New World's most distant frontier. Beginning in 1769 with the founding of a fortress and a Franciscan mission at San Diego, and culminating in 1776 with the founding of another outpost at what is now San Francisco, a series of small but self-reliant religious colonies was established, each a day's travel apart and linked by El Camino Real, The King's Highway, a route followed roughly by today's US-101.

Some of the most interesting missions are listed below, north to south, followed by the dates of their founding.

**San Francisco Solano de Sonoma (1823).** The only mission built under Mexican rule stands at the heart of Sonoma, a history-rich Wine Country town.

**San Juan Bautista (1797).** This lovely church forms the heart of an extensive historic park, in the town of the same name (see page 90).

**San Carlos Borromeo (1770).** Also known as **Carmel Mission,** this was the most important of the California missions (see page 96).

**San Antonio de Padua (1771).** This reconstructed church, still in use as a monastery, stands in an undeveloped valley inland from Big Sur in the middle of Hunter Liggett Army base. Monks still live, work, and pray here, making for a marvelously evocative visit (see page 103).

**San Miguel Arcangel (1797).** The only mission not to have undergone extensive renovations and restorations—almost everything, notably the vibrantly colorful interior murals, is as it was.

**La Purisima Mission (1787).** A quiet coastal valley is home to this church, which was restored in the 1930s using traditional methods as part of a New Deal employment and training project (see page 112).

**Santa Barbara (1782).** Called the Queen of the Missions, this lovely church stands in lush gardens above the upscale coastal city (see page 114).

**San Gabriel Arcangel (1771).** Once the most prosperous of the California missions, it now stands quietly and all but forgotten off a remnant of Route 66 east of Los Angeles.

**San Juan Capistrano (1776).** Known for the swallows that return here each year, this mission has lovely gardens, but the buildings have been badly damaged by earthquakes and the elements; they've been under scaffolding for years (see page 130).

**CALIFORNIA MISSIONS (1769 - 1823)**

San Francisco Solano de Sonoma (1823)

San Rafael (1817)

San Francisco de Asis (1776)

Santa Clara (1777)

San Jose (1797)

PACIFIC OCEAN

Santa Cruz (1791)

San Juan Bautista (1797)

San Carlos Borromeo (1770)

Soledad (1791)

San Antonio de Padua (1771)

San Miguel Arcangel (1797)

San Luis Obispo de Tolosa (1772)

La Purisima Concepcion (1787)

Santa Ynez (1804)

Santa Barbara (1782)

San Buenaventura (1782)

San Fernando Rey (1797)

San Gabriel Arcangel (1771)

San Juan Capistrano (1776)

San Luis Rey (1798)

San Diego (1769)

El Camino Real

0       50 miles

0       50 kilometers

UNITED STATES
MEXICO

look at the gift shop, which sells postcards of the different rooms. Guys should head down to the men's room, where the urinal trough is flushed by a waterfall.

Though the Madonna Inn has a huge, banquet-ready restaurant—done up in white lace and varying hues of pink—the best places to eat are located downtown, near the mission. **Linnaea's Cafe** (805/541-5888), at 1110 Garden Street off Higuera, serves coffee and tea and sundry snack items all day and night; there's also the lively, veggie-friendly **Big Sky Cafe** (805/545-5401) at 1121 Broad Street, and the usual range of beer-and-burger bars you'd expect from a college town.

A pedestrian walkway in downtown San Luis Obispo, off Higuera Street between Garden and Broad Streets, has become known around the world as **Bubble Gum Alley**. Since the 1950s, local kids have written their names and allegiances on the brick walls, using chewing gum rather than the more contemporary spray paint.

Along with the Madonna Inn, San Luis has a number of good places to stay, with reasonable rates that drop considerably after the summertime peak season. Besides the national chains, try the **Peach Tree Inn,** 2001 Monterey Street ($80 and up; 805/543-3170), or the **La Cuesta Inn** ($80 and up; 805/543-2777 or 800/543-2777), at 2074 Monterey Street. There's also the **HI-San Luis Obispo Hostel** (805/544-4678), near downtown and the Amtrak station at 1617 Santa Rosa Street.

Also worth noting: Every Thursday evening, the main drag of San Luis Obispo, Higuera Street, is closed to cars and converted into a very lively farmers market and block party, with stands selling fresh food and good live bands providing entertainment.

## Pismo Beach

South of San Luis Obispo, Hwy-1 and US-101 run along the ocean past **Pismo Beach** (pop. 8,551), a family-oriented beach resort where the main attraction is driving or dune-buggying along the sands. Pismo was once famous for its clams, now over-harvested to the point of oblivion, but you may still see people pitchforking a few small ones out of the surf. The area has grown significantly in the past decade, thanks mainly to an influx of retired people housed in red-roofed townhouses, but Price Street, the old main road, offers a wide range of motels and fast-food restaurants.

Every winter, a grove of trees just south of downtown Pismo Beach (west of Hwy-1, just north of Grand Avenue) turns into a prime gathering spot for migrating monarch butterflies. This is one of the largest populations in the country, numbering over 25,000 in recent years. At the south end of Pismo Beach, **Nipomo Dunes State Preserve** holds endless acres of sand dunes and marshlands, as well as the buried remains of a movie set used in Cecil B. DeMille's *The Ten Commandments*.

## Guadalupe and Santa Maria

South of Pismo Beach, the highways diverge. Hwy-1 cuts off west through the still-agricultural areas around sleepy **Guadalupe** (pop. 5,659), where produce stands sell cabbages, broccoli, and leafy green vegetables fresh from the fields. The town itself feels miles away from modern California, with a four-block Main Street lined by Mexican cafés, bars, banks, and grocery stores. A great place to get a feel for Guadalupe is at the **Far Western Tavern** (805/343-2211), open daily for breakfast, lunch, and dinner at 899 Guadalupe Street. Try the barbecued tri-tip steaks, which are awesome.

In the late 1930s, Nipomo was the place where **Dorothea Lange** took that famous photograph of a migrant mother huddling with her children in a farm-worker camp.

If you opt to follow US-101, shopping malls and tract-house suburbs fill the inland valleys through **Santa Maria,** a town best known these days for the sad saga of pop star Michael Jackson. Before Wacko Jacko's child-abuse trials, however, Santa Maria was famous for its thick cuts of salsa-slathered barbecued beef, which can be sampled at the large and historic **Santa Maria Inn** (805/928-7777), a half mile west of US-101 at 801 S. Broadway. Completing our tour of great Santa Maria-area barbecue places is **Jocko's** in Nipomo, east of US-101 at Tefft Street to 125 N. Thompson Avenue (805/929-3686), where great steaks (and mouth-wateringly moist, inch-thick barbecued pork chops!) highlight the all-day, no frills menu.

## Lompoc and La Purisima Mission

The rolling valleys around Lompoc are famed for their production of flower seeds, and consequently the fields along Hwy-1 are often ablaze in brilliant colors. Apart from colorful murals adorning downtown buildings, **Lompoc** as a town is not up to much, despite the unusual nature of the area's two main nonagricultural employers. One is a minimum-security federal prison; the other is Vandenburg Air Force Base, site of numerous missile tests, the aborted West Coast space shuttle port, and the $60 billion "Son of Star Wars" National Missile Defense program.

With its long arcade reaching across the floor of a shallow, grassy valley, **Mission La Purisima** (daily; $4 per car; 805/733-3713) gives a strong first impression of what the missions may have looked like in their prime. Four miles northeast of Lompoc, between Hwy-1 and US-101 on Hwy-246, the mission here was originally built in 1812 but fell to ruin before being totally reconstructed as part of a WPA makework scheme in the New Deal 1930s. During the restoration, workers used period techniques wherever possible, hewing logs with hand tools and stomping mud and straw with their bare feet to mix it for adobe bricks. Workers also built most of the mission-style furniture that fills the chapel and the other rooms in the complex. Also here: a functioning aqueduct, many miles of hiking trails, and a small museum.

## Buellton and Solvang

The town of **Buellton,** a block west of US-101 at the Solvang exit, holds one of California's classic roadside landmarks, **Andersen's Pea Soup Restaurant** (805/688-5581), advertised up and down the coast. Another Buellton landmark, the **Hitching Post** restaurant (805/688-0676), starred in the wine-loving road-trip movie, *Sideways.*

Four miles east of Buellton and US-101, America's most famous mock-European tourist trap, the Danish-style town of

**Solvang** (pop. 5,332) was founded in 1911. Set up by a group of Danish immigrants as a cooperative agricultural community, Solvang found its calling catering to passing travelers. The compact blocks of cobblestone streets and Old World architecture, highlighted by a few windmills and signs advertising the Hamlet Motel among many more suspicious claims to Danishness, now attract tourists by the busload. Many other U.S. towns (Leavenworth, Washington, and Helen, Georgia, to name two) have been inspired by Solvang's success, but to be honest there's nothing much to do here apart from walking, gawking, and shopping for pastries.

Just east of Solvang's windmills and gables, the brooding hulk of **Mission Santa Ynez** stands as a sober reminder of the region's Spanish colonial past. Built in 1804, it was once among the more prosperous of the California missions, but now is worth a visit mainly for the gift shop selling all manner of devotional ornaments.

Pop singer Michael Jackson's Neverland Ranch lies here in the foothills of the Santa Ynez Valley, southeast of Solvang via the truly scenic Hwy-254, which loops inland south to Santa Barbara.

## Gaviota and Refugio State Beaches

Between Solvang and Santa Barbara, US-101 follows the coast past some of California's most beautiful beaches. Dropping through a steep-sided canyon, US-101 reaches the coast at **Gaviota State Beach,** where a small fishing pier and campground are overwhelmed by the massive train trestle that runs overhead. Continuing south, US-101 runs atop coastal bluffs past prime surfing beaches, usually marked by a few VWs pulled out along the west side of the highway. Midway along this stretch of coast, some 22 miles north of Santa Barbara, **Refugio State Beach** has groves of palm tress backing a clear white strand. There's also a small, summer-only store, and a number of attractive campsites with hot showers.

**Rancho del Cielo,** the ranch of former President **Ronald Reagan,** spreads along the crest of the coastal hills above Refugio State Beach.

Reservations for camping at Gaviota or Refugio, or at any

California state beach, should be made in advance by calling 800/444-7275.

## Santa Barbara

The geographical midpoint of California may well be somewhere near San Francisco, but the Southern California of popular imagination—golden beaches washed by waves and peopled by blond-haired surfer gods—has its start, and perhaps best expression, in Santa Barbara. Just over 100 miles north of Los Angeles, **Santa Barbara** (pop. 92,325) has grown threefold in the last 60 years, but for the moment, at least, it manages to retain its sleepy seaside charm. Much of its character comes from the fact that, following a sizable earthquake in 1929, the town fathers—caught up in the contemporary craze for anything Spanish Revival—required that all buildings in the downtown area exude a mission-era feel, mandating red-tile roofs, adobe-colored stucco, and rounded arcades wherever practicable. The resulting architectural consistency gives Santa Barbara an un-American charm; it looks more like a Mediterranean village than the modern city that, beneath the surface, it really is.

For a good first look at the city head down to the water, where **Stearns Wharf** sticks out into the bay, bordered by palm tree–lined beaches populated by joggers, in-line skaters, and volleyball players. From the wharf area, follow State Street away from the sands to the downtown district, where Santa Barbarans parade among the numerous cafés, bars, and boutiques. At the north end of downtown is the excellent **Museum of Art** (closed Mon.; $9, free Sun.; 805/963-4364), at 1130 State Street. A block east on Anacapa Street, the **County Courthouse** is one of the finest public buildings in the state, a handcrafted Spanish Revival monument set in lush semitropical gardens, with an observation tower (daily 9 AM–5 PM; free) giving a fine view over the red-tiled cityscape.

Santa Barbara's reigning attraction, **Mission Santa Barbara** (daily; $5; 805/682-4713), stands atop a shallow hill a well-posted mile up from State Street, looking out over the city and shoreline below. Called the "Queen of the Missions" by the

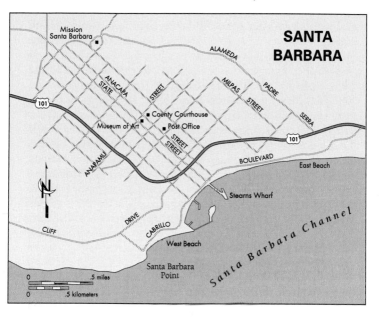

local tourist scribes, Mission Santa Barbara is undeniably love-ly to look at, its rose-hued stone facade perfectly complement-ed by the roses and bougainvillea that frame the well-maintained gardens and lawns.

Santa Barbara has perhaps the coast's best variety of places to eat. State Street holds the most lunch and dinner places, like the old-fashioned burgers and beer on tap in the dark-wood dining room of **Joe's Cafe** (805/966-4638) at 536 State Street. Great Italian food at fair prices has made a favorite of **Ca' Dario,** just off State at 37 E. Victoria Street (805/884-9419), while some of the world's best hole-in-the-wall Mexican food is served a half mile east of State Street at **La Super-Rica** (805/963-4940) at 622 N. Milpas Street, where such distinguished foodies as Julia Child have come to chow down on a vari-ety of freshly made soft tacos and deli-cious seafood tamales. It's not cheap, but the food is great (fresh tortillas, traditional *adobado*-marinated pork, and spicy chori-zo), and the *horchata* is the creamiest you'll taste. Yum.

Santa Barbara is one of many great places along the coast to go on a **whale-watching cruise,** on the *Condor Express* or other boats, to see migrating gray whales in winter and jumping humpbacks in summer. Trips take a half day or full day, and some head out to the Channel Islands; call 805/963-3564 or 888/779-4253 for details or reservations.

The city's accommodations, however, are among the central coast's most expensive, especially in summer when even the most basic motel can charge as much as $150 a night. One of the nicest of many motels is the **Franciscan Inn** ($90 and up; 805/963-8845), just a short walk from the beach and wharf at 109 Bath Street. At the top of the scale, the **Simpson House** ($275 and up; 805/963-7067 or 800/676-1280) at 121 E. Arrellaga Street offers comfortable, centrally located B&B rooms. Off the scale completely, money's-no-object visitors can enjoy the deluxe facilities of the **San Ysidro Ranch** ($750 and up; 805/969-5046), in the hills above neighboring Montecito, where Jackie and JFK spent some of their honeymoon. Somewhat ironically, considering the generally high prices here, international budget chain Motel 6 got its start in Santa Barbara, where it now has five properties, including one near the beach at 443 Corona Del Mar ($80; 805/564-1392).

## Channel Islands National Park

South of Santa Barbara, US-101 widens into an eight-lane free-way along the coast. Looking out across the Pacific, beyond the partially disguised off-shore oil wells, you can't miss seeing the sharp outlines of the Channel Islands, whose rocky shores are protected as
a national park. Consisting of eight islands altogether, they sit from 12 to nearly 50 miles off the mainland. Numerous scenic cruises around the Channel Islands start from Santa Barbara, but only the smallest and closest, Anacapa Island, is easily accessible to the public, via daily trips from Ventura Harbor, offered by **Island Packers** ($42; 805/642-1393).

## Ventura

Midway between Malibu and Santa Barbara, **Ventura** (pop. 100,916) is an offbeat little place, its three-block Main Street lined by enough thrift shops (seven at last count) to clothe a destitute retro-minded army. Apart from searching out vintage couture, the main reason to stop is the small and much-reconstructed **Mission San Buenaventura** (daily; donations), standing at the center of Ventura at 225 E. Main Street, just east of the US-101 freeway. This was the ninth in the California mission chain, and the last one founded by Father Junípero Serra, in 1782. A block from the mission at 113 E. Main Street, the **Albinger Archaeological Museum** (closed Mon.; free) collects a wide range of artifacts—the oldest from 1500 BC, the most recent from early American settlers—all excavated from a single city block–sized site alongside the mission.

Ventura doesn't get anything like the tourist trade that Santa Barbara draws, but it does have the very pleasant **Bella Magiore Inn** ($90 and up; 805/652-0277 or 800/523-8479), offering good-value B&B rooms in a nicely restored 1920s courtyard house at 67 S. California Street, between downtown and US-101.

South of Ventura, US-101 heads inland through the San Fernando Valley to Hollywood and downtown Los Angeles, while Hwy-1 heads south through the 10 miles of stop-and-go sprawl that make up the rapidly suburbanizing farming community of **Oxnard** (pop. 170,358), then continues right along the coast through Malibu and West Los Angeles.

> Ventura is the birthplace and headquarters of the outdoor equipment and clothing company **Patagonia,** started and still owned by legendary rock climber **Yvon Chouinard.**

## Simi Valley

If you opt to follow US-101 rather than coastal Hwy-1 into Los Angeles, be sure to check out the somnolent suburb of **Simi Valley,** 20 miles east of Ventura, where the hilltop **Ronald Reagan Presidential Library** (daily; $12; 805/522-2977) fills 150,000 square feet of Spanish-style stucco with a fascinating array of exhibits and artifacts, most famously a chunk of the Berlin Wall, set in a Cold War–era tableau. Also here, housed in a 200-foot-long glass-walled pavilion, is the actual Boeing 707 used as presidential Air Force One by Nixon, Carter, and Reagan. The "Great Communicator" was interred here following his death in 2004; to get to the library, take US-101 to Hwy-23 North (a.k.a. the Ronald Reagan Freeway), exit at Olsen Road, and follow the signs.

The other Simi Valley sight to see is **Bottle Village** (donations; 805/583-1627), a complex of small buildings and sculptures built out of glass bottles, TV sets, hubcaps, and assorted other recycled refuse in the 1940s and 1950s by the late Tressa Prisbey. Subject of a heated battle between folk-art preservationists and those who think it's a pile of junk, the "village" can be viewed at 4595 Cochrane Street, a mile south of the Hwy-118/210 freeway between the Tapo Canyon and Sterns Road exits.

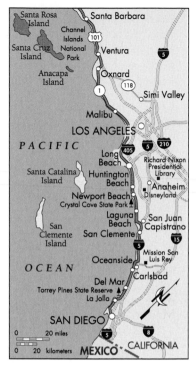

## Pacific Coast Highway Beaches

Running right along the beach, the Pacific Coast Highway (Hwy-1) heads south from Oxnard around the rocky headland of **Point Mugu** (ma-GOO), where the U.S. Navy operates a missile testing center and the Santa Monica Mountains rise steeply out of the Pacific Ocean. Most of these chaparral-covered granite mountains have been protected as parkland, with hiking, cycling, and riding trails offering grand views and a surprising amount of solitude. Before or after a hike in the hills (or a Harley ride along the coast, the preferred mode of arrival), the ramshackle **Neptune's Net** restaurant (310/457-3095) at 42505 Pacific Coast Highway is a great place to hang out and "star"-gaze while enjoying fresh seafood, served up on paper plates for that down-home Hollywood feel.

South from here, a series of state-owned beaches marks your progress along the coastal road, but this stretch is basically natural wilderness—apart from the highway, of course. Biggest and best of the beaches hereabouts is the lovely **Leo Carrillo State**

**Beach** (818/880-0363), which has a sandy strand, some great tidepools, and a sycamore-shaded campground (reservations 800/444-7275). Leo Carrillo (1880–1961) was an actor (he played Pancho in *The Cisco Kid* TV show) and preservationist who was instrumental in expanding the California state parks.

South of Leo Carrillo, which marks the Los Angeles County line, there are many more public beach areas, including (in roughly north-to-south order) Nicholas Canyon County Beach, El Pescador, El Matador (where episodes of TV's *Baywatch* have been filmed). At big, brash Zuma Beach, where volleyball courts and snack bars line the sands, the PCH highway bends inland around the headlands of Point Dume, a great spot for winter whale-watching.

## Malibu

South of Zuma Beach, houses begin popping up along Hwy-1 to block the oceanfront views, and more-elaborate multimillion-dollar homes dot the canyons above as well, forming the sprawling exurbia and movie-star playground of **Malibu,** which stretches along Hwy-1 for the next 27 miles into Santa Monica and metropolitan Los Angeles. Unless TV helicopters are flying overhead to document the latest wildfire or other natural disaster, it's hard to get more than a glimpse of the garage doors or wrought-iron gates of these palaces, but this is the address of choice for the movers and shakers of the entertainment world: If you can name them, they probably own property here. Most of the truly huge estates are hidden away on ranches high up in the mountains.

> The main route inland from the coast, Malibu Canyon Road, was the setting of the key murder scene in James M. Cain's thriller *The Postman Always Rings Twice.*

One of these hideaways has been evolving since 1993, when Barbra Streisand donated her 22-acre ranch for use as a botanical preserve. Called **Ramirez Canyon Park,** and located at 5750 Ramirez Canyon Road, it's managed by the Santa Monica Mountains Conservancy and is sometimes open to visitors (but usually not, thanks to complaints from the neighbors).

From Hwy-1, the most prominent sight is the **Pepperdine University** campus, which was described by the late, great architect Charles Moore as "an overscaled motel set in obscenely vivid emerald lawns." Below the bluff-top campus, the legendary **Malibu Colony** of celebrity homes stretches along the coast in high-security splendor.

About the only place in Malibu where it's fun (and legal) to explore is the area around the landmark **Malibu Pier,** which juts into the ocean at the heart of Malibu's short and rather scruffy commercial strip. North of the pier, which was used most famously in TV's *The Rockford Files,* stretches **Surfrider Beach,** site of most of those Frankie Avalon and Annette Funicello *Beach Blanket Bingo*–type movies made during the 1950s. The pier and the beach are part of **Malibu Lagoon State Park,** which also protects the historic **Adamson House,** 23200 Pacific Coast Highway (Wed.–Sat. 11 AM–2 PM; $5; 310/457-8185), a lovely old circa-1929 Spanish Revival court-yard home, right on the beach and full of gorgeous tile work and other architectural features. Tours of the house are given throughout the day, and fascinating exhibits portray Malibu history and the Rindge family, who once owned the entire region.

Just north of the pier and the Adamson House, another great place to get a feel for Malibu is at **Malibu Seafood,** 25653 PCH (310/456-3430), a low-key beach shack drawing local gardeners and Hollywood starlets for BYOB fish-and-chips.

## Topanga and the Getty Villa

Between Malibu and Santa Monica, **Topanga Canyon** is one of the last great wild spaces in Los Angeles, with a number of parks, trails, and perhaps the last wild and free waterways— steelhead trout still spawn in the waters of Topanga Creek, which flows down from the mountains to the Santa Monica Bay. Home to an alternative-minded community of some 5,000 hippies and New Agers since the 1960s (when Neil Young recorded *After the Gold Rush* in his home here), Topanga was first established as an artists' colony by the likes of Woody Guthrie and actor Will Geer, who played Grandpa in TV's *The Waltons,* long after he'd been blacklisted during the anti-Communist McCarthy witch-hunts. For the past 30 years Geer's old property has been preserved as the **Theatricum Botanicum,** a garden and politically minded 300-seat open-air theater, six miles up the canyon at 1419 N. Topanga Canyon Blvd (310/455-2322).

South of Topanga, and once again open to the public after a 10-year, $275-million remodeling, are the world-famous an-tiquities of the **J. Paul Getty Museum.** Over 1,200 priceless classics are displayed in the pseudo-Pompeiian Getty Villa, where the oil magnate's art collection was housed prior to the construction of the massive Getty Center complex above Brentwood. Admission to the Getty Villa is free, but parking reservations ($8 per car; 310/440-7300) are essential.

From the Getty Villa south to Santa Monica, the Pacific Coast Highway (Hwy-1) runs along the wide-open sands of **Will Rogers State Beach,** gifted to the public by the Depression-era humorist.

## Crossing Los Angeles

From Malibu and Topanga Canyon, Hwy-1 swoops along the shore, running along the beach as far as the landmark Santa Monica Pier before bending inland through a tunnel and metamorphosing quite unexpectedly into the I-10 Santa Monica Freeway. The second exit off this freeway (which has been officially dubbed the Christopher Columbus Transcontinental Highway, running all the way east to Jacksonville, Florida) takes you to Lincoln Boulevard, which carries the Hwy-1

Since Hwy-1 follows slow-moving Lincoln Boulevard and other surface streets across L.A., if you are in any sort of hurry you should stay on the Santa Monica Freeway (I-10) east to the San Diego Freeway (I-405), and follow that south as far as you're going. Coming from the south, follow these freeways in reverse order—or risk the time-consuming consequences.

moniker south through Venice and Marina del Rey to Los Angeles International Airport (LAX), where it runs into Sepulveda Boulevard.

After passing through a tunnel under the airport runways—worth the drive just for the experience of seeing 747s taxiing over your head—Sepulveda emerges in the Tarantino-esque communities of L.A.'s "South Bay," which utterly lack the glamour of chichi Santa Monica and Malibu. At Hermosa Beach, one of a trio of pleasant if surprisingly blue-collar beach towns, Sepulveda Boulevard changes its name to Pacific Coast Highway, then bends inland to bypass the ritzy communities of the Palos Verdes Peninsula, passing instead through the industrial precincts of San Pedro that border the Los Angeles/Long Beach harbor, one of the busiest on the West Coast.

## Long Beach

Directly south of downtown Los Angeles, the city of **Long Beach** (pop. 461,522) is the second-largest of L.A.'s constituent cities, but it feels more like the Midwest than the cutting-edge West Coast. Long Beach is probably best known as the home

# Los Angeles

Love it or hate it, one thing you can't do about L.A. is ignore it. Thanks to Hollywood in all its many guises (movies, television, the music industry), the city is always in the headlines. Without falling too deeply under the spell of its hyperbole-fueled image-making machinery, it's

safe to say that L.A. definitely has something for everyone. In keeping with its car-centered culture, however, our suggested tour ignores the many individual attractions and focuses instead on a pair of quintessential L.A. drives.

Winding along the crest of the Hollywood Hills, **Mulholland Drive** is the classic L.A. cruise. Starting in the east within sight of the Hollywood Sign and the Hollywood Bowl, this ribbon of two-lane blacktop passes by the city's most valuable real estate, giving great views on both sides, both by day and after dark.

Another classic L.A. cruise, running from the scruffy fringes of downtown all the way west to the coast, **Sunset Boulevard** gives glimpses into almost every conceivable aspect of Los Angeles life. Starting downtown, the historic core of colonial Los Angeles and now a showcase of contemporary architecture thanks to a stunning new cathedral and concert hall, Sunset Boulevard's 27-mile course then winds west past Echo Park and Hollywood to West Hollywood, where it becomes the Sunset Strip, still the liveliest nightclub district in town. Continuing west, Sunset winds through Beverly Hills, Brentwood, and Bel-Air, lined by the largest mansions you're likely to see, before ending up at the edge of the Pacific Ocean.

## Practicalities

Most flights into Los Angeles arrive at Los Angeles International Airport (LAX), on the coast southwest of downtown, where you'll find all the usual shuttles and rental car agencies. Other useful L.A. airports include Bob Hope (BUR) in Burbank, and John Wayne (SNA), in Orange County.

Before choosing a place to stay, think about where you want to spend your time and settle near there. High-end places abound, but character can be hard to come by. Along the coast, recommended accommodations range from the handy **Santa Monica HI Hostel** ($25 per person; 310/393-9913), a block from the beach at 1436 2nd Street, to the unique **Hotel Queen Mary** in Long Beach ($109 and up; 562/435-3511), offering authentic art deco–era staterooms in the fabulous old luxury liner. Mid-range with a great mid-city location, try the **Farmer's Daughter** ($149 and up; 800/334-1658), next to the historic Farmer's Market at 115 S. Fairfax Avenue, a very friendly 1950s-style motel with tons of charm and the city's hottest new shopping mall and entertainment complex, The Grove, across the street. Downtown, the most fabulous place to stay is the retro-1960s **Downtown Standard,** 550 S. Flower Street ($175 and up; 213/892-8080), with the world's coolest rooftop, poolside bar.

For food, one place I always try to stop is the **Apple Pan** (310/475-3585), at 10801 W. Pico Boulevard, an ancient (circa-1947) landmark on the West L.A. landscape, serving the best hamburgers on the planet—though I'll admit to being biased, since I grew up eating them. Take a seat at the counter, and be sure to save room for a slice of the wonderful fruit pies. Late at night, the huge sandwiches and heart-warming soups at **Canter's Deli,** 419 N. Fairfax Avenue (open daily 24 hours; 213/651-2030), draws all kinds of night owls to a lively New York–style deli in the heart of the predominantly Jewish Fairfax District. Downtown, in the heart of old L.A. at 1001 Alameda, **Philippe's French Dip Sandwiches** (213/628-3781) is a classic working man's cafeteria, offering good food at impossibly low prices, with character to spare.

The **Los Angeles Dodgers** (323/224-1471) play at beautiful Dodger Stadium, on a hill above downtown.

The usual array of information about hotels, restaurants, tickets to TV show tapings, and all other L.A.-area attractions is available through the **Los Angeles Convention and Visitors Bureau** (213/689-8822 or 800/228-2452), with an office at 685 S. Figueroa Street.

of the cruise ship RMS *Queen Mary,* one of the largest and most luxurious liners ever to set sail. Impossible to miss as it looms over Long Beach harbor, the stately ship is open for self-guided tours ($25; 562/435-3511). You can also stay overnight in one of the many staterooms and

cabins, traveling back to a more elegant time for surprisingly reasonable overnight rates.

In place of Howard Hughes's famous "Spruce Goose" airplane, which used to stand next door, there's now a Cold War–era submarine, and across the bay on the main downtown Long Beach waterfront, the **Aquarium of the Pacific** (daily; $20.95; 562/590-3100) explores the diverse ecosystems of the Pacific Ocean, from tropical coral reefs (shown off in an amazing, 360,000-gallon display) to the frigid waters of the Bering Sea. The tanks full of jellyfish of all kinds, colors, and sizes are the main event.

Other Long Beach attractions include the **world's largest mural,** a 115,000-square-foot painting of migrating gray whales on the outside of the Long Beach Arena, and the self-proclaimed **Skinniest House in the USA,** at 708 Gladys Avenue.

Long Beach also marks the southern end of L.A.'s reborn streetcar and subway system, and you can ride the Blue Line north to downtown. It's an inexpensive base for exploring the Los Angeles area, especially if you avail yourself of the **HI-South Bay Hostel** (310/831-8109), on a hill overlooking the harbor area at 3601 S. Gaffey Street. There's also a **Best Western** ($120 and up; 562/599-5555) at 1725 Long Beach Boulevard, directly across from a Blue Line train stop.

## Huntington Beach

Winding south and east from Long Beach, Hwy-1 continues along the coast past a series of natural marshlands and small-craft marinas. The first real point of interest is the town of **Huntington Beach** (pop. 189,594), one of the largest communities in Orange County. Founded in 1909 by Henry Huntington as a stop along his legendary Pacific Electric "Red Car" interurban railway network, Huntington Beach is best known as one of the places where **surfing** really took off on the U.S. mainland. To attract Angelenos down to his new town, Huntington hired Hawaiians to demonstrate the sport, which at the time made use of huge solid wooden boards, 15 feet long and weighing around 150 pounds. Huntington Beach, especially around the pier, is still a very popular surfing spot—though contemporary surfers slice through the waves on high-tech foam-core boards, a third the size of the original Hawaiian long boards. The history and culture of West Coast surfing, with examples of boards then and now (plus special collections highlighting surf movies and the creation of surf music by local heroes Leo Fender and Dick Dale), is recounted in the fantastic **International Surfing Museum** (daily noon–5 PM; donations; 714/960-3483), two blocks from the pier at 411 Olive Avenue, in the heart of the lively downtown business district.

## Disneyland

Like a little bit of middle America grafted onto the southern edge of Los Angeles, inland Orange County used to feel like a totally different world. Though the area's demographics have changed considerably

**The Los Angeles Angels of Anaheim** (714/940-2000) play at Angel Stadium at 2000 E. Gene Autry Way.

in the past decade or two, becoming more a part of L.A.'s fast-paced, edgily creative multiethnic stew, Orange County in the 1950s and 1960s was suburban America writ large—mostly white, mostly well-off, and absolutely, totally bland. In short, a perfect place to build the ultimate escapist fantasy, the self-proclaimed "Happiest Place on Earth," **Disneyland.**

The phenomenon of Disneyland has been done to death by all sorts of social critics, but the truth is, it can be great fun—provided you visit out of season and get there early to avoid the crowds, and really immerse yourself in the extroverted, mindless joy of it all. (Being here in the company of appreciative 8- to 12-year-olds is probably the best way to maximize your enjoyment.)

If you haven't been before, or not for a while at any rate, here are some useful tidbits of information: Disneyland is 20 miles south of downtown L.A., right off I-5 in the city of

Anaheim—you can see the Matterhorn from the freeway. The park is open daily; in summer, it remains open until midnight. Admission to the park, which includes all rides, costs around $70 per person per day, with discounts for extended visits; kids under 9 save $10. For further park details, including operating hours, call Disneyland at 714/781-7290.

Disneyland opened in 1955, when there was nothing surrounding it; in intervening years, an entire metropolis has grown up around it. In 2001 the park was joined by the much smaller, more grown-up—oriented **California Adventure** theme park. Instead of cuddly cartoon characters, this billion-dollar park has thrill rides like California Screamin', a 60-mph roller coaster, and the excellent Soaring Over California motion simulator, offering an airborne tour of the Golden State from Yosemite Falls to the Malibu beaches. California Adventure is separate from Disneyland, but a "Park Hopper" pass allows entry into both for just a few dollars more than a one-park admission. California Adventure hours are shorter than Disneyland's, opening later in the summer and closing earlier year-round.

The whole Disney ensemble includes an upscale resort-hotel complex, surrounded by motels and yet more motels, and it is well worth staying overnight so you can get an early start, go "home" for a while, then come back for the nightly fireworks show. A highly recommended place to stay is the **Sheraton Park Hotel** ($120 and up; 714/750-1811), a block from Disneyland at 1855 S. Harbor Boulevard, offering spacious modern rooms (and a nice pool), with free parking and free shuttles every half hour to and from Disneyland.

## Richard Nixon Presidential Library

If you've already done the Disneyland thing, or just want a foil to the empty-headed fun, there is one other Orange County attraction you really shouldn't miss: the **Richard Nixon Presidential Library** (daily; $9.95; 714/993-5075), at 18001 Yorba Linda Boulevard, 10 miles northeast of Disneyland off Hwy-91. The library is built on the very ground where the former president was born in 1913; It's also where he and his wife, Pat, are buried, side by side next to the restored Craftsman-style bungalow where Nixon grew up. No matter what your feelings toward him, the spare-no-expense displays do a fascinating job of putting his long career into the distorted perspective you'd expect from the only president ever forced to resign from office. Highlights are many, such as the pictures of the pumpkin patch where Whittaker Chambers concealed the microfilm that Nixon used to put Alger Hiss in prison as a Communist spy, next to photos of Nixon and JFK as chummy freshman U.S. senators sharing sleeping compartments on a train. The best-selling item in the gift shop? Postcards of Nixon greeting Elvis Presley, also available as mousepads, china cups, and fridge magnets.

## Newport Beach

Back on the coast, if you want to get a sense of what wealthy Orange Countians do to enjoy themselves, spend some time along the clean white strands of **Newport Beach.** Located at the southern edge of Los Angeles's suburban sprawl, Newport started life in 1906 as an amusement park and beach resort at the southern end of the L.A. streetcar lines. Since then thousands of Angelenos have spent summer weekends at the **Balboa Pavilion,** at the southern tip of the slender Balboa peninsula, where the "Fun Zone" preserves a few remnants of the pre–video game amusements—a Ferris wheel, a merry-go-round, and those odd "Pokerino" games in which you win prizes by rolling rubber balls into a series of numbered holes.

Midway along the peninsula, near 23rd Street, Newport Pier is flanked by another holdout from the old days: the **dory fleet.** For more than a century small boats have set off from the beach here (often around midnight, landing back around 7 AM) to catch rock cod and more exotic fish, which are sold fresh off the boats at an outdoor market right on the sands.

A mile south of Balboa Pavilion, next to the breakwater at the very southern end of Balboa peninsula, **The Wedge** is one of the world's most popular and challenging bodysurfing spots, with well-formed waves often twice as high as anywhere else on the coast.

To return to Hwy-1 from Balboa Peninsula, you can either backtrack around the harbor or ride the **Balboa Ferry,** which shuttles you and your car from the pavilion across the harbor past an amazing array of sailboats, power cruisers, and waterfront homes.

## Crystal Cove State Park

Midway between Newport and Laguna Beaches, amidst the ever-encroaching Orange County sprawl, **Crystal Cove State Park** (daily dawn–dusk; $10 per car; 949/494-3539) protects one of Southern California's finest chunks of coastline. With three miles of sandy beaches and chaparral-covered bluff lined by well-marked walking trails, it's a fine place to enjoy the shoreline without the commercial trappings. Originally home to Native Americans, the land here was later part of Mission San Juan Capistrano and, until 1979 when the state bought it, the massive Irvine Ranch, which once covered most of Orange County.

The main parking area for Crystal Cove is at **Reef Point** near the south end of the park, where there are bathrooms and showers plus excellent tidepools, a fine beach, and a well-preserved collection of 1920s beach cottages, where you can stay overnight ($75–150; 800/444-7275). There is also a large section of the park inland from Hwy-1, through the oakland glade of **El Moro Canyon,** which gives a vivid sense of Orange County's rapidly vanishing natural landscape.

## Laguna Beach

Compared with much of Orange County, **Laguna Beach** (pop. 23,727) is a relaxed and enjoyable place. Bookstores, cafés, and galleries reflect the town's beginnings as an art-

tableau from Laguna Beach's
Pageant of the Masters

ists' colony, but while the beach and downtown area are still very attractive, the surrounding hills have been covered by some of the world's ugliest tracts of "executive homes."

During the annual **Pageant of the Masters,** Laguna Beach residents re-create scenes from classical and modern art by forming living tableaux, standing still as statues in front of painted backdrops. Held every summer, it's a popular event and proceeds go to good causes, so get tickets ($15–80; 949/497-6582 or 800/487-3378) well in advance.

Right across Hwy-1 from the downtown shopping district, which is full of pleasant cafés and a wide range of art galleries, Laguna's main beach (called simply Main Beach) is still the town's main draw, with a boardwalk, some volleyball courts, and a guarded swimming beach with showers.

Many other fine but usually less crowded and quieter beaches are reachable from Cliff Drive, which winds north of downtown Laguna past cove after untouched cove; follow the signs reading Beach Access.

Laguna Beach has a number of nice places to eat; one place worth searching out is the small **Taco Loco** (949/497-1635), at 640 S. Hwy-1 at the south end of the downtown strip, where the ultra-fresh Mexican food includes your choice of three or four different seafood tacos, from shark to swordfish, in daily-changing specials from about $2 each.

Places to stay are expensive, averaging around $150 a night, and include the beachfront **Laguna Riviera Hotel and Spa,** 825 S. Hwy-1 (949/494-1196). At the top end of the scale, the newish **Montage Resort,** 30801 S. Hwy-1 (866/271-6953), is California's only Mobil five star–rated spa and resort, with everything you could want from a hotel—all yours for $750 a day (and up!).

South of Laguna Beach, Hwy-1 follows the coast for a final few miles before joining up with the I-5 freeway for the 40-mile drive into San Diego.

## San Juan Capistrano

Of the 21 missions along the California coast, **Mission San Juan Capistrano** (daily; $6; 949/234-1300) has been the most romanticized. When the movement to restore the missions and preserve California's Spanish colonial past was at its apogee in the late 1930s, its main theme tune was Leon Rene's "When the Swallows Come Back to Capistrano," popularizing the legend that these birds return from their winter migration every St. Joseph's Day, March 19. After wintering in Goya, Argentina, they do come back to Capistrano, along with several thousand tourists, but the swallows are just as likely to reappear a week before or a week after—whenever the weather warms up, really.

The mission, which has lovely, bougainvillea-filled gardens, stands at the center of the small, eponymously named town, a short detour inland along I-5 from the coast. Besides the birds, the main attractions include the small **chapel,** the last surviving church where the beatified Father Serra said Mass, widely considered the oldest intact church and perhaps the oldest building of any kind in California, and the ruins of the massive **Stone Church,** a finely carved limestone structure that collapsed in an earthquake in 1812, just six years after its completion. Many visitors to the chapel are terminally ill patients saying prayers to St. Pereguin, the patron saint of medical miracles.

To get a sense of the huge scale of the Stone Church, a full-sized replica called the New Church has been constructed behind the mission and now serves as the official mission church, open to visitors except during religious services. Across the street from the New Church, a Michael Graves–designed local **library** gives an intriguing postmodern take on the mission style.

In the block between the historic Mission and the I-5 freeway, the Walnut Grove Restaurant and Mission Inn Motel are two of the few survivors of old-style San Juan Capistrano, holding out against the relentless suburbanizing that has leveled many of the surrounding historic commercial structures. Bridging old and new worlds, the **Mission Inn Motel** has been upgraded into a boutique B&B ($175; 949/234-0249), mixing old-fashioned charm with modern comforts. Another unique spot is the **Coach House** (949/496-8930), two miles south of the mission at 33157 Camino Capistrano, one of Southern California's best small clubs for listening to live music.

## San Clemente

At the southern tip of coastal Orange County, **San Clemente** marks the midway point between San Diego and Los Angeles. A sleepy beachside community, with frequent Amtrak train service and a nicely undulating stretch of old US-101 (El Camino Real) running through its heart, San Clemente is probably best known as the site of Casa Pacifica, the one-time "Western White House" of former president Richard Nixon, who lived here following his election in 1968 until after his impeachment in the mid-1970s. The white-walled, mission-style house at the south end of Avenida del Presidente (the western frontage road to I-5) is more easily visible from the beach below, though the 25 acres of trees have grown up to obscure it in recent years.

Within a quick walk uphill from the handful of cafés and bars on and around the pier, **The Beachcomber** ($150 and up; 949/492-5457) is a tidy, old-fashioned motor-court motel, facing onto the open ocean. San Clemente also has a handy **HI Hostel** (949/492-2848), just a short walk from the beach at 233 Avenida Granada, and a great breakfast and burger place: **Duke's Griddle N Grill,** 204 S. El Camino Real (949/492-8822) in the mission-style downtown business district.

## Mission San Luis Rey de Francia

In the sun-bleached hills above the blue Pacific, four miles east of the ocean off the I-5 along Hwy-76, **Mission San Luis Rey de Francia** (daily; $5) was among the largest and most successful of the California missions.  Its lands have been taken over by Camp Pendleton, and most of the outbuildings have disappeared, but the stately church at the heart of the complex survives in fine condition, worth a look for the blue-tinted dome atop the bell tower and for the haunting carved stone skull that looks down from the cemetery gate.

A long but worthwhile detour inland from San Luis Rey brings you to the least visited but perhaps most evocative of all the California missions, **Mission San Antonio de Pala** (sometimes closed Mon.; $2; 760/742-1600). Located on the Pala Indian Reservation, 20 miles east of San Luis Rey along Hwy-76, then another 100 yards north along a well-marked side road, Mission San Antonio de Pala is the only California mission still serving its original role of preaching to the native people, and it gives an unforgettable impression of what California's mission era might have been like.

## Oceanside

At the southern edge of 125,000-acre Camp Pendleton Marine Corps Base, **Oceanside** (pop. 161,029) is the largest city between Los Angeles and San Diego, but it offers little to attract the casual visitor—apart from guided tours of Camp Pendleton's amphibious-assault training exercises, and the state's longest fishing pier. But if you're in the mood to shop for camouflage gear, watch the muscle cars cruise Hill Street, get a $5 G.I. Joe haircut, or drink beer with a gang of young recruits, this is the right place.

Oceanside is also home to one of the last survivors of the old, pre–I-5, Coast Highway businesses: The **101 Café** (760/722-5220) at 631 S. Coast Highway has been open for classic road food since 1928; it often hosts classic car rallies and generally glows with neon-lit nostalgia.

The northwest corner of San Diego County is taken up by the U.S. Marines Corps's massive **Camp Pendleton** training base, which fills 125,000 acres, running for 20 miles along the coast and 15 miles inland. Camp Pendleton (the base motto is "No Beach out of Reach") is the largest undeveloped section of the Southern California coast.

South from Oceanside, all the way to San Diego, a very pleasant alternative to the often-clogged I-5 is the old alignment of US-101, now signed as County Road S21 (and occasionally, Coast Highway 101). Slower than the freeway but still in regular use, the old road is now the main drag of quaint beachfront towns like Carlsbad, Leucadia, Encinitas, and Del Mar. If you have the time, it's a great drive, in sight of the ocean for most of the way.

## Carlsbad: La Costa and Legoland

Named for the European spa town of Karlsbad, in Bohemia of what's now the Czech Republic, **Carlsbad** (pop. 78,247) was established in the 1880s and had a half-century heyday as a spa town and vacation resort. A few remnants of the historic resort area still survive along old US-101 in the center of town.

A few flower and strawberry fields surround the town, surviving against the ever-expanding tide of sprawl, and these days Carlsbad's spa-town heritage lives on at **La Costa Resort and Spa** ($275 and up; 760/438-9111), a 500-room complex of luxurious rooms, health spas, golf courses, and tennis courts covering 400 acres of hills on the inland side of I-5.

Some of the best views of the Southern California coastline can be had from the windows of the frequent **Coaster commuter trains,** which run right along the shore between Oceanside and downtown San Diego.

Carlsbad's other main attraction is the first American outpost of the popular European children's theme park **Legoland** (adults $60, children $50; 760/918-5346). Built out of more than 30 million Lego bricks, and covering 128 acres above the Pacific Ocean, the park is divided up into three main areas, including MiniLand, where miniature landscapes modeled on New York, New Orleans, New England, and the Northern California coast have all been constructed using the trademark plastic bricks.

model of San Francisco made entirely from Lego blocks

**South Carlsbad State Park** ($8 per car; 760/438-3143) three miles south of town, is one of the nicest and most popular places to camp on the Southern California coast, with its spacious campsites with hot showers ($20–25) spread out along a sandstone bluff above a broad beach. However, swimming can be dangerous because of strong riptides. If you don't want to camp, or pay the parking fee, leave your car at the park entrance, which is well marked on a surviving stretch of the old US-101 highway.

# San Diego

Set along a huge Pacific Ocean harbor at the southwestern corner of the country just a few miles from the Mexican border, San Diego embodies the Southern California ideal. Around the turn of the 20th century, it rivaled Los Angeles as a boomtown based on wild real estate

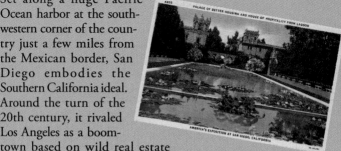

speculation, but while L.A. continued to expand by leaps and bounds, San Diego grew comparatively slowly. Instead of Hollywood glamour, San Diego's economy has long been based on the U.S. Navy, as evidenced by the massive former USS *Midway* moored right downtown. (San Diego successfully mixed its military and Hollywood influences in the movie *Top Gun*.) Despite a metropolitan population of nearly 3 million people, San Diego still feels small and anything but urban.

The main things to see in San Diego are in **Balboa Park,** a lushly landscaped 1,150-acre spread on downtown's northwest edge, which was laid out and constructed as part of the 1915 International Exposition celebrating the completion of the Panama Canal. The many grand buildings, all built in gorgeous Spanish Revival style by architect Bertram Goodhue, have been preserved in marvelous condition, and now house sundry museums, ranging from automobiles to fine art to a functioning replica of Shakespeare's Globe Theatre.

Balboa Park is also home to the **San Diego Zoo** (daily; $35; 619/234-3153), one of the largest and most popular in the world with over 4,000 animals kept in settings that simulate their natural habitats. You can see koalas and komodo dragons, panda bears and polar bears, plus gorillas, giraffes—you name it, if it's anywhere outside in the wild, it'll be here amidst the zoo's lushly landscaped 100 acres.

## Practicalities

The city of San Diego bends diagonally around its natural harbor, which makes orientation occasionally confusing. The main airport, Lindbergh Field, is on the waterfront just north of downtown—and has one of the swiftest final approaches of any urban American airport. Because it is small and relatively compact, San Diego is easy to get around. Downtown is walkable, and on a bike you could see most everything in a day. Buses operated by San Diego Transit (619/234-1060) fan out from downtown, while the light rail Tijuana Trolley runs south from downtown to the Mexican border.

The **San Diego Padres** (619/795-5000) play at retro-modern Petco Park, right downtown in the Gaslamp Quarter.

Though you may feel the need to duck when planes land at nearby Lindbergh Field, for breakfast try the **Hob Nob Hill** (619/239-8176) at 2271 First Avenue, a classic 1940s coffee shop with great pecan waffles. For more all-American fare, head west to Ocean Beach, where **Hodad's,** a great old burger joint awaits you at 5010 Newport Avenue (619/224-4623). San Diego's Old Town historic park holds some good old-school Mexican places, like the **Old Town Café,** at 2489 San Diego Avenue (619/297-4330). In Balboa Park, soak up San Diego's Spanish Revival splendor while enjoying a meal at **Prado** (619/557-4441) in the original House of Hospitality.

Places to stay are generally modern, clean, and comfortable, though rates vary with seasons (and conventions). For top-of-the-line accommodations, or just to appreciate the historic architecture, head to the wonderful old **Hotel Del Coronado** ($250 and up; 619/435-6611), across the bridge from downtown on Coronado Island at 1500 Orange Avenue. Rising up in turreted glory, this fabulously grand Victorian-era resort hotel still caters, as it always has, to the four-star trade. It has been seen in many movies, including the great Peter O'Toole flick *The Stunt Man.* It's also where England's King Edward VIII first met the femme fatale who inspired him to give up his throne: Mrs. Wallis Simpson, whose husband was commander of the local navy base. The cheapest beds are at the **HI San Diego Hostel** ($25 per person; 619/525-1531), in the historic downtown Gaslamp Quarter at 521 Market Street, or the hip **500 West** ($89 and up; 619/234-5252), a boutique restoration of a 1920s YMCA at 500 West Broadway. For more comfort and character, try the **Hotel Sofia,** a recently restored 1920s hotel at 150 W. Broadway ($135 and up; 800/826-0004). For surfer-friendly accommodations near Ocean Beach and Point Loma, try the **Ocean Villa Motel** at 5142 W. Point Loma Boulevard ($90 and up; 619/224-3481).

The best range of information is available from the **San Diego Visitors Center** (619/236-1212) at 1040 W. Broadway.

## Del Mar and Torrey Pines State Reserve

Most of the time, **Del Mar** (pop. 4,860) is a sleepy little upscale suburb of San Diego, with big houses backing onto a fine, four-mile-long beach. But in late summer, it comes to life for the thoroughbred racing season at beautiful **Del Mar Racetrack,** built by Hollywood types like Bing Crosby, and seen in *The Grifters* and many other Hollywood movies. The waves here are well suited to bodysurfing, but the sands can be hard to reach in summer because of a lack of parking—weekdays it's less of a problem.

A Torrey Pine, San Diego, Cal.—9

South along the Camino Del Mar coast road from Del Mar, hang-gliders, tidepoolers, surfers, and beachcombers flock to the nearly 2,000 acres of bluffs and beaches protected in **Torrey Pines State Reserve.** Named for the long-needled pines that grow naturally only here, the reserve is crisscrossed by hiking trails leading down steep ravines between the bluffs and the sands. Besides hang-gliders, Torrey Pines is prime air space for remote-controlled model gliders, which float gracefully in the nearly constant onshore breeze. The primary launching spot is the small city park at the south end of the reserve.

Overlooking the Pacific from atop a bluff at the south end of the reserve, the **Salk Institute** is one of the world's most important centers for research in the life sciences. Founded by the late Jonas Salk, designed by Louis Kahn, and modeled in part on the gardens of the Alhambra in Granada, the institute is open for **tours** Monday–Friday at 10 AM, 11 AM, and noon (free; 760/453-4100).

Stretching inland and south from the Salk Institute, the hills are covered with faceless business parks around the spacious campus of **University of California at San Diego** (UCSD), beyond which spreads La Jolla and the greater San Diego area. At the southwest edge of the campus, learn all about local marine biology at the **Birch Aquarium** of UCSD's Scripps Institute ($11; 858/534-FISH), from where you can amble along the shore to lovely La Jolla.

## La Jolla

The wealthiest and most desirable part of San Diego, La Jolla sits along the coast northwest of the city proper, gazing out over azure coves to the endless Pacific. Besides the gorgeous scenery, great surfing (head to Windansea for the best waves), beachcombing, and skin diving, a big draw here is the recently renovated **Museum of Contemporary Art** (daily; $6; 858/454-3541), overlooking the ocean at 700 Prospect Avenue. Tons of good cafés and restaurants have long made La Jolla an all-around great day out, suiting all budgets—especially those with no upper limit.

Pacific Beach, one of Southern California's better surfing spots, is home to the friendly, family-run **Pascowitz Surf Camp** (949/728-1000), held every summer since 1972.

Start the day off right at La Jolla's **Cottage** (858/454-8409), at 7702 Fay Avenue, where delicious food (including a divine buttermilk coffee cake) is served up on a sunny patio. For a memorable lunch or dinner, the very plush **Tapenade** (858/551-7500) at 7612 Fay Avenue is one of the best restaurants in Southern California, offering a deluxe mix of Mediterranean dishes. To continue the swaddled-in-luxury SoCal experience, stay the night at the elegant, Craftsman-style **Lodge at Torrey Pines** ($299 and up; 858/453-4420), a modern re-creation of California's turn-of-the-20th-century Golden Age located at 1148 N. Torrey Pines Road.

At **Belmont Park,** west of Mission Bay at 3146 Mission Boulevard (619/491-2988), the **Giant Dipper** wooden roller coaster survives as the sole remnant of a 1920s beachfront amusement park.

## Driving San Diego

From La Jolla south, the US-101 highway is pretty well buried by the I-5 freeway. Old US-101 can still be followed, however, by following Pacific Highway past Mission Bay and Lindbergh Field toward San Diego Bay, where it becomes Harbor Drive—where the light rail Tijuana Trolley now runs.

# Index

# Photo and Illustration Credits

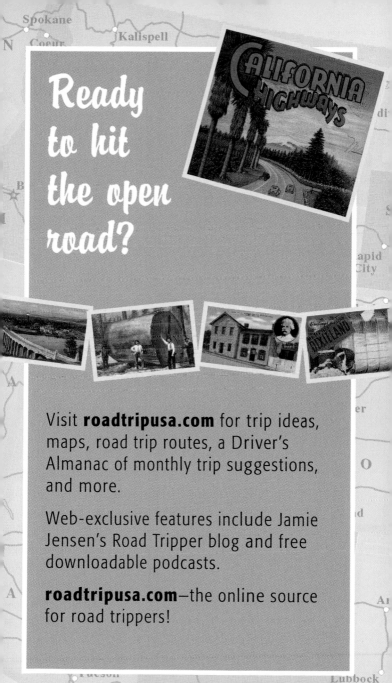

# www.moon.com

**MOON.COM** is all new, and ready to help plan your next trip! Filled with fresh trip ideas and strategies, author interviews, informative blogs, a detailed map library, and descriptions of all the Moon guidebooks, Moon.com is all you need to get out and explore the world—or even places in your own backyard. As always, when you travel with Moon, expect an experience that is uncommon and truly unique.

**ROAD TRIP USA**
**Pacific Coast Highway**
1st Edition

Jamie Jensen

Avalon Travel
a member of the Perseus Books Group
1700 Fourth Street
Berkeley, CA 94710, USA
www.travelmatters.com

Printing History
1st edition — 2009
5 4 3 2 1

Printed in the United States by RR Donnelley

ISBN-13: 978-1-59880-204-7
ISSN: 1946-3278

Editor: Elizabeth Hollis Hansen
Graphics Coordinator: Jane Musser
Production Coordinator: Darren Alessi
Map Editor: Kevin Anglin
Cartographers: Kat Bennett, Mike Morgenfeld, Suzanne Service
Indexer: Judy Hunt